WARTIME NEW FOREST REVEALED

WARTIME NEW FOREST REVEALED

JOHN LEETE

Bourchier Books

Published by

Bourchier Books

ISBN 978-0-9934692-9-9

Copyright © John Leete, 2017
The moral right of the author has been asserted

All rights reserved. Without limiting the rights under copyright reserved above, no part of this publication may be reproduced, stored in or introduced into a retrieval system, or transmitted in any form or by any means (electronic, mechanical, photocopying, recording or otherwise), without the prior written permission of both the copyright holder and the above publisher of this book

A CIP catalogue record for this book is available from the British Library

Typeset and designed by
Russell Wallis
RJW|Creative Design,
5 Priory Terrace, Cheltenham, Gloucestershire, GL52 6DS
www.rjwcreativedesign.co.uk

Printed in Great Britain by
Short Run Press Ltd, Bittern Road,
Sowton Industrial Estate, Exeter, EX2 7LW
01392 211909
info@shortrunpress.co.uk
www.shortrunpress.co.uk

This book is dedicated to Katy Priddis

CONTENTS

Foreword — ix
Preface — xi
Acknowledgements — xv
Abbreviations — xvii
Introduction — xix

....

Chapter 1	Past, Present and Future	1
Chapter 2	The First Christmas	11
Chapter 3	The Tide of War	19
Chapter 4	Watching and Waiting	35
Chapter 5	Hands Across the Sea	45
Chapter 6	Each Man Gave of His Best	55
Chapter 7	A Long Battle in the Skies	65
Chapter 8	In This Great Struggle	83
Chapter 9	Called to Arms	101
Chapter 10	A Day in the Life	121
Chapter 11	The New Forest at War Revealed	137
Chapter 12	To Conserve and Enhance	161

....

Postscript — 171
References — 177
Wartime Sites — 181
The Unseen Legacy — 195

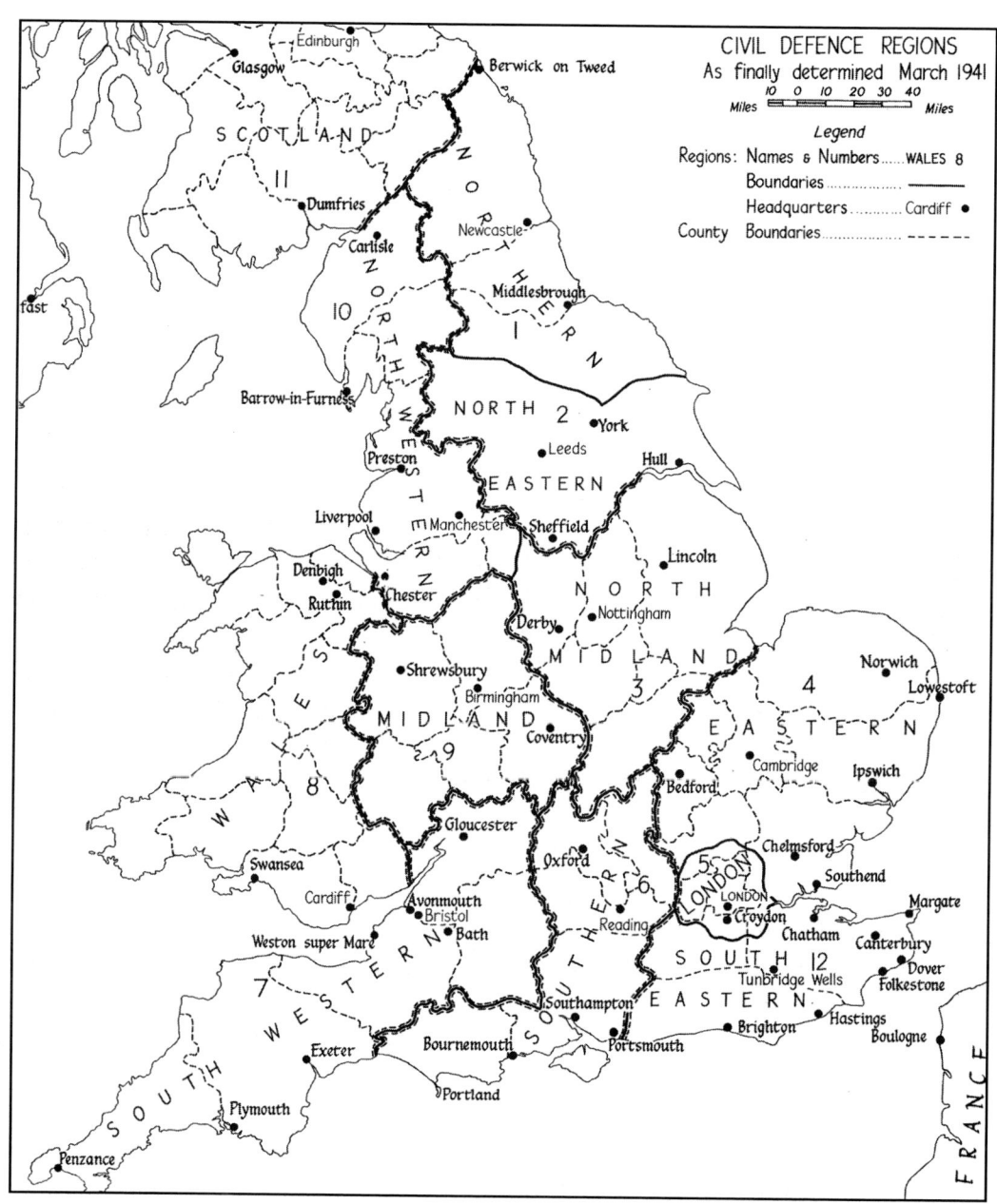

The New Forest was designated Area 6 Civil Defence Region. (Author's collection)

FOREWORD

The history of the Second World War is well documented and written about, and we are lucky that it is so. At no other time in our own lives have we been able to find out so much about what happened, with as much detail and in so many forms as we can today.

Films, LiDAR surveys, maps, aerial photography, personal accounts and military archives, for example, all help to give us a new dimension to our recent history. *The New Forest at War Revealed* is a book that adds one more piece to this fascinating jigsaw. The author, John Leete, is a journalist, writer and historian who has dedicated much of his working life to researching and writing about Britain's Home Front history.

The incredible drama that took place in the New Forest involved the entire local population as well as tens of thousands of Service personnel and others, who came here to take part in the war effort. It had a significant impact on the area of course, not just socially, but also in terms of the massive infrastructure which served the Armed Forces. The Forest, thankfully, has returned to the wonderful environment we see today.

Leete's book gives us an insight into what happened here in such an excellent and fascinating way that I shall never again be able to travel through the area without recalling the incredible stories and events he writes about in a most brilliant manner.

WARTIME NEW FOREST REVEALED

For the now tranquil Forest, which today welcomes millions of visitors from home and overseas, was once the hub of military operations, not least ahead of and up to the launch of D-Day in 1944.

Here begins your voyage of discovery, which I know you will find enthralling.

Oliver Tobias
Director and documentary film-maker
www.olivertobias.co.uk

PREFACE

I started working for the New Forest National Park Authority in 2009 as an education and outreach officer on the Coastal Heritage Project, whilst finishing a Masters in Maritime Archaeology at Southampton University. Archaeology has always been a passion for me and something I have enjoyed and worked in since leaving school. The role as an education and outreach officer on an archaeological project was a new and engaging challenge that I was keen to put my mind to, as I wanted to share my passion and interest with others. The Heritage Lottery Funded Coastal Heritage Project was a great success, with a huge response to our education resources, talks, interpretation, website and underwater film. This success helped secure further partnership funding for a new project: *New Forest Remembers – Untold Stories of World War II*, which I took on the challenge of managing. The Second World War is a very important aspect of our heritage, and though there is a huge amount of historical interest and detailed specific independent research, little overall archaeological surveying had been carried out in the New Forest. As such, the area is a classic example of the paradox recognised by English Heritage that some of our most recent history and archaeology is fast becoming our rarest, as research focuses on older periods and evidence continues to be removed and forgotten. The New Forest Remembers project was a chance to reverse this trend, and to try to produce a more accurate record of what was happening in the New Forest during the Second World War, capture personal memories of the Forest and champion the work being undertaken by individuals and groups. The success of the information gathering that was undertaken has seen a tenfold jump in public archaeology records for the Second World War, but it is not just a recording exercise. Dealing with the war provides us with an opportunity to capture personal memories, photos and documents, which can all be used to enhance the archaeological record. It is true that lots of information relating to the war still exists, but a lot of the material is in disparate archives, and work is required to link it all together and ensure long-term preservation. This is unique in an archaeological project: we have the potential to interview individuals who were based in the New Forest area and to add layers of additional detail to the sites we are studying. This provides us with a perfect opportunity to engage visitors, residents and future generations with what might appear to be just a lump of concrete: a site that someone might pass off as rubbish can be understood for its important history and the human connection made, making it easier for visitors to relate to, and connect with it, and hopefully ensuring its future protection. This is what we are working to achieve with the New Forest Remembers Interactive Portal and the mobile phone application we are developing to support it.

James Brown, New Forest Remembers Project Manager
www.newforestnpa.gov.uk/wwii
New Forest National Park Authority

For many people, the word archaeology instantly conjures up an image of Time Team digging trenches in sunny fields and discovering a plethora of fascinating artefacts. Yet behind any sort of archaeological investigation is a substantial amount of preparation and research. Nowadays, any sort of fieldwork is usually preceded by an archaeological Desk-Based Assessment (or DBA).

A DBA is conducted to assess the extent and potential of the archaeological resource in a given area. Simply put, it is an opportunity to identify and review all of the existing research material on a site, so that when any fieldwork is done the archaeologists and historians have the best possible idea of what to expect. A DBA may be done in advance of the building of a new housing estate, or even for the construction of something as small as a house extension. The DBA for the New Forest Remembers project was quite different; the overall study area was just over 1,000km². Fortunately, this massive study area was tempered somewhat by the smaller study period. A DBA is usually concerned with all periods of history, from the Stone Age through to the Cold War. I was therefore quite lucky that the study period for the New Forest Remembers project was so narrow (1935–47).

Nonetheless, the DBA would need to cover many hundreds of individual locations where Second World War activity took place, ranging in scale from the construction of an airfield to the digging of a slit trench. The research involved a wealth of sources, from Luftwaffe aerial photographs and period unit war diaries to modern LiDAR mapping and up-to-date national monuments lists.

A DBA of this size required a means of compiling all the data in one place. The most straightforward way of doing this was to construct a database into which information, sources and grid references of each identified site could be entered. The database could also be loaded into modern GIS mapping systems, allowing the sites to be visualised on a New Forest map. As each source of information became available, it was reviewed, and relevant information was entered into the database. The information derived from existing databases (predominantly the National Monuments Record, county Historic Environment Records, the Defence of Britain Database and the National Mapping Project), contributions from local groups and societies (including the Beaulieu Estate and Friends of New Forest Airfields) and other sources, including archaeological reports and books, eventually identified 1,500 unique sites in the Forest. In many instances this did not even account for the many smaller elements of one site (such as the numerous individual buildings that make up one camp). Additionally, research into unit war diaries (a record kept by every unit active during the war) and historic maps identified some 600 other locations that were previously unrecorded or totally unknown.

Of these, some 120 sites were selected to be included in the DBA, therefore warranting extra attention from the New Forest Remembers team. These include sites that are well preserved, unique or unusual facilities, and those that demonstrate the potential to provide more information from fieldwork.

The DBA was a thoroughly enjoyable text to write (all 54,000 words of it). As well as giving an extensive background to the overall role of the Forest during the war and the activities that took place, the history of each of the 120 sites was thoroughly researched and a full assessment of their importance and potential was produced. I'm particularly pleased to have contributed in this way to the New Forest Remembers project.

Stephen Fisher, Maritime Archaeology Trust
www.maritimearchaeologytrust.org

ACKNOWLEDGEMENTS

I am indebted to the team at the New Forest National Park Authority upon whose original wartime memories project and mapping surveys this book is partially based. Without that support, and the kind contributions from and support of many other individuals and organisations, this book would not have been possible.

I would like to extend my sincere thanks to everyone listed below. The list is alphabetical, rather than in any particular order of preference. If I have missed anyone, please accept my sincere apologies. Every effort has been made to trace copyright holders and obtain permission to reproduce material. Please contact the publisher if any details have been inadvertently overlooked, and corrections will be made in any future editions.

The family of Chris Ashworth
Alison Barnes
Ian Bayley
Emma Blake
James Brown
Nick Catford
Sally Collier
Neville Cullingford
Mat Dickson
Mike Ellis
Dave Fagan, Hampshire Airfields
Stephen Fisher, Maritime Archaeology Trust
Paul Francis

Frank Green
Doug Gregory
Nick Halling
Hampshire Women's Institute at County HQ
Laura Joyner
Kimberley Keay
Maxine Knott
Laura Lawton
John Leavesley
Ann Mattingly
New Milton Memorial Centre – in particular Michelle and Phyllis
Old English Inns
Gareth Owen
Hazel Robinson
Lawrence Shaw
Martin and Chris Simmonds
Staff at Hurst Castle
Tom Sykes, Coleshill Auxiliary Research Team (CART) – especially for Chapter 9
Oliver Tobias
Andrew Walmsley
Will Ward
Amberley Books, for permission to quote from *Brothers in Arms*, John Leete and Brian Berringer (2015)

John Leete, 2017

ABBREVIATIONS

AA – Anti-Aircraft
ADS – Archaeological Data Service
AFS – Auxiliary Fire Service, also Army Fire Service
AHBR – Archaeology & Historic Buildings Record
ARP – Air Raid Precaution
AU – Auxiliary Unit
FONFA – Friends of New Forest Airfields
GIS – Geographic Information System
GPS – Global Positioning System
HCC – Hampshire County Council
HER – Historic Environment Record
HLS – Higher Level Stewardship
HMS – His Majesty's Ship
LDV – Local Defence Volunteers
LiDAR – Light Detection and Ranging
NFDC – New Forest District Council
NFNPA – New Forest National Park Authority
NFS – National Fire Service
NMP – National Mapping Programme
NRHE – National Record of the Historic Environment
NT – National Trust
OP – Observation Post
PLUTO – Pipe Line under The Ocean
RAF – Royal Air Force
RCZA – Rapid Coastal Zone Assessment
RNAS – Royal Navy Air Service
SMR – Scheduled Monument Record
SOE – Special Operations Executive
UKHO – United Kingdom Hydrographic Office
USAAF – United States Army Air Force
WO – War Office

WHAT MIGHT HAPPEN IN WAR

It is probable that in an air attack on this country an enemy would make use of fire bombs. The object would be not only to destroy property but also to create panic.

A large number of these bombs might be dropped in a small space. A large proportion of them would fall in gardens, streets and open spaces where they would burn out without doing much damage. But in a built-up area some would fall on the roofs of houses. One of these houses might be YOURS.

HOME FIRE FIGHTERS.

However strong the Fire Brigade may be, an outbreak of many fires all close together and beginning at the same time would be more than it could successfully deal with *unless the householder himself and his family took the first steps in defending their home.*

In Civil Defence EVERYBODY has a part to play. This is specially true of fire-fighting. In every house there should be one or more people ready to tackle a fire bomb. So read what follows ; read it again and again, make the preparations which are advised and see that everyone in your house knows exactly what to do. Then you will be able to protect your own home and the homes of your neighbours. For once a fire gets out of control you cannot tell how fast it may spread. All large fires start as small ones.

THE FIRE BOMB

The ordinary fire bomb is not in the least like a high explosive bomb. It may weigh as little as two pounds or so. It may not explode at all, but will blaze up and may scatter burning material in all directions.

It will go through any ordinary house roof if dropped from sufficient height, but a small bomb will probably come to rest on the first boarded floor below the roof. Fires will therefore mostly break out in roof spaces, attics and upper storeys.

For a time after a bomb has blazed up it may be impossible to get near it, and all that can be done will be to keep the fire from spreading. But when the bomb has burnt for about a minute it should be possible to get near enough to get the bomb under control before it does further mischief.

HOW TO DEAL WITH A FIRE

There will be two things to deal with—the bomb itself and the fire or fires it has started. Each of these may have to be tackled in different ways, but the main thing is to prevent the fire from spreading.

Every household received instructional leaflets like this. (Author's collection)

INTRODUCTION

In remembering the legacy of the New Forest at war, we must first consider the Forest, its people, its wartime contribution and the climate on the road to war during the latter half of the 1930s.

The legacy is built upon this foundation, and so this book sets the scene through personal anecdotes, period news items, details of the state of the nation and aspects of wartime preparations. However, it is by no means an exhaustive account of the New Forest during the Second World War or its social and built legacy.

The Forest, a military training area since the sixteenth century, had a pivotal role during the preparations for and the launch of D-Day in 1944. Many consider that the ultimate success of the D-Day campaign was in part because the Allied Armed Forces were able to harness so much power and might within the Forest. This coastal location was deemed ideal geographically and an almost purpose-built springboard from which to launch a major component of Operation Overlord.

With over 100,000 troops under canvas, twelve airfields, 3,000 available aircraft, 7,000 vehicles, thousands of tons of stores and equipment, and up to 5,000 ships and various other craft lying at anchor in the Solent, along Southampton Water, the Beaulieu River and at other moorings, the Forest was at the forefront of a turning point in world history.

In 1939, just a generation after the First World War ended, Britain was plunged into conflict again. The Munich Agreement of a year earlier had bought much-needed time to prepare. By the time war broke out, preparations had affected every citizen, town and village, and aspect of day-to-day life.

From as early as 1937, and throughout the period of the so-called 'phoney war', men and women were mobilised in their thousands, children were evacuated, factories requisitioned for war production, air raid shelters built and gas masks issued. There was much more besides. The whole nation was swept by tides of preparation, resolution and grim determination.

In the New Forest, as in other parts of the country, mobilisation was carried out with a mix of efficiency and confusion. Instructions changed almost on a daily basis, local officials were left to interpret the instructions as they saw fit, and natural leaders, many with knowledge of the First World War, had to make the best of the situation. However, because the coastline of Hampshire and the New Forest was close to mainland Europe, the authorities in the area did not miss the need for a much more vigorous approach to preparation and defence.

The interior of a shelter on Ibsley Common. (RAF Ibsley Historical Group)

INTRODUCTION

As people prepared themselves for life on the Home Front, so the armed services and emergency services applied themselves to the mechanics of war. The New Forest had been used for military training even before the First World War, and from 1939 and for the duration of the war this was constant, culminating in the assembly of men and machines for D-Day in 1944. In 1935 the population was a little over 26,000 (divided into three administrative areas: Lymington, Ringwood and New Forest District), but this increased to over 130,000 at its peak.

After Dunkirk and the Battle of Britain, the early planning for what was later to be known as D-Day began to manifest itself at locations across the Forest. The Army, Royal Navy and Royal Air Force (RAF) all requisitioned country estates. For example, Breamore House near Fordingbridge became a base for both British and American personnel, and General George Patton was stationed there for a short time. The Pylewell Estate near Lymington was already being used by the military, and it then served as a landing ground for the United States Army Air Force (USAAF). The Beaulieu Estate, the home of the Montague family, became one vast military establishment. The training of the Special Operations Executive (SOE) took place here and naval craft were built on the Beaulieu River. Various regiments and units were camped across the estate, while an airfield was built 2 miles away alongside the main road to Lymington.

The Exbury Estate, which adjoins Beaulieu, became a Royal Navy shore establishment, known as HMS (also referred to in the Services as His Majesty's Stone Frigate) Mastodon, and legendary in many respects, not least for its association with Nevil Shute and for being the site of the shooting down of a low-flying and over-crewed German aircraft – mystery surrounding the event remaining to this day. In October 1940 the 1 regiment Compagnie de l'infanterie de l'air, Free French Forces was based here and later it was used by Free Polish Special Forces employed in Operation Bardsea. This was designed to use agents drawn from Monika (Poland) as paratroopers specialising in sabotage and subversive activities in specific operations just behind the bridgeheads on D-Day.

Great tracts of land across the Forest were used as training camps, tank driving schools, army camps, anti-aircraft gun sites, rifle ranges, mobile fire

Butchers Field airstrip, close to Breamore House. (Edward Hulse)

One of the SOE finishing schools at Beaulieu. (Beaulieu Estate)

INTRODUCTION

Marion Loveland, a former WRNS, was originally based at nearby HMS Collingwood. She has been the driving force behind the Exbury Veterans Association. (Exbury Veterans Association)

Landing craft, a number of which were crewed by personnel from HMS Mastodon, Exbury. (Exbury Veterans Association)

xxiii

stations, stores and ammunition depots. Later, airfields were constructed on many sites from Hurn (now Bournemouth International Airport) in the west to Beaulieu Heath in the east. Calshot air station, further east, was already established as a flying boat base. Debris and remains of some of these airfields and advance landing grounds (ALGs) can be found.

Large houses were turned into hospitals, prisoner-of-war camps were erected, Air Raid Precautions (ARP) and Fire Service Centres were created and Local Defence Volunteers (LDV, later Home Guard) units were formed. The Forest was now the focus of much financial and practical input by civilian and armed services. Archive footage available at the Wessex Sound and Film Archive in Winchester shows some of the frantic activity that ensued. The building of new roads and the widening of existing routes, the felling of trees for the airfield construction programme, and later the creation of tented cities to house the thousands of troops that moved into the area in the months before D-Day, all warranted the need for 20,000 workers across the Forest at the peak of the programme.

As the war progressed, there were many recorded incidents of civilians being strafed by German aircraft and bombs being dropped right across the Forest, Allied aircrews killed in action were buried in Forest churchyards. Rationing was in force, although many Forest folk were able to supplement their diets by living off the land. There was always the black market too, and later in the war, when the Americans arrived, generous food parcels filtered out into local communities.

New friendships were forged, and by 1942 the Forest had become a vast cosmopolitan community. In addition to the Americans, there were men from Canada, Pakistan, Ireland, India, Australia, New Zealand, Poland, South Africa, Czechoslovakia and France (members of the Free French Army). Rumours were rife about the reasons for the long and sustained influx of men and machines from early 1944, especially as security was becoming noticeably tighter: many local people recalled how they were unable to visit certain parts of the Forest at all, and even those areas that it was possible to access were very heavily policed. From all of the airfields, bombers and fighters flew many sorties in the days before 5 June (the original date for D-Day).

INTRODUCTION

Fireboats in Southampton Water. (HFRS)

Combat training intensified for the troops, and planning intensified too. There was time for recreation, but it was a nervous fun that these men experienced. Southampton Water and the Solent were full of ships (records suggest between 4,000 and 5,000, but many smaller craft were attached to larger vessels and may not have been included in some of the counts). Great wartime leaders, including Churchill, Montgomery and Eisenhower, visited many of the numerous planning centres across the Forest, as did King George VI, who was said to have been particularly fascinated by the work being undertaken at Exbury.

Then instructions came for the embarkation. There was a state of heightened readiness, and archive newsreel footage captured the scene at some of the embarkation points – many men looking directly at the camera and smiling enthusiastically. It is a glimpse of that moment in history when the fate of the whole world was in the hands of those few men.

Within days of the assault on Fortress Europe, the Forest was almost deserted. Fewer sorties were flown from the airfields, and the camps emptied as wave after wave of troops left to support the post D-Day campaign. Many requisitioned properties were quickly handed back to their owners, and the roads were empty of all but a few military vehicles. It was eerily quiet. Gradually the Forest returned to normality, and although the war in Europe (and the Far East) would last for another year, the people here were now as optimistic as they were elsewhere in the country.

Today, the Forest welcomes millions of both day and stay visitors from home and from overseas, making it one of Europe's major visitor destinations. In stark contrast to those turbulent days of 1939 to 1945, the Forest is tranquil, a place of recreation, relaxation and leisure. This has only been made possible by the sacrifice of many and the determination of all. It is fitting that All Saints' Church, Fawley, is dedicated to all the servicemen and women who were stationed in the New Forest, and in this book we remember those who gave their lives so that our generation and future generations can enjoy the Forest and its rich natural landscape, its wildlife and its heritage.

This book chronicles a number of recent discoveries and newly researched aspects of the Second World War history of the Forest, with social commentary and anecdotes reflecting regional demands and operational climates. By no means is it likely that the story will ever be known or told in full, because every day another piece of the giant jigsaw of history is discovered. However, this contribution will, I hope, permit us to better understand our past and to treasure our heritage.

1

Past, Present and Future

In the immediate pre-war years, Britain was undergoing changes socially as well as in its industries and its technological capabilities. In the 1930s, the country was finally throwing off the legacy of the First World War, yet it was still trying to cope with the Depression (also known as the Great Slump).

High unemployment levels began to decrease during 1934, and two years later they decreased significantly when the government simultaneously embarked on road-building and ship-building projects to stimulate growth. The inter-war years' programme for building airfields (known variously as an expansion programme and an emergency planning project) also created work from the mid-1930s.

Underpinning the social changes was the availability of news, not just through the newspapers, but crucially via the radio (or the wireless as it was known), which was widely accessible throughout the country, mainly thanks to the BBC. Whilst in many ways the radio service was still in its infancy, it quickly became an integral part of the day-to-day lives of most folk, to the extent that by the outbreak of war, and for the duration, the radio played a crucial role in keeping the mind and soul of the nation together. It was also a powerful propaganda weapon.

The newly built Broadcasting House, standing proud and shining white against a rainy December morning in 1932, was a sight to behold with its modern art deco curves, majestically cast Portland stone, floor to ceiling windows on the ground floor and its array of exterior sculptures. Inside, the new paint and polished wood of the corridors were reminiscent of a luxury ocean liner, and every detail from the lights to the door handles had been carefully considered to ensure that the building was as cutting edge as the technology it was designed to accommodate.

In Studio 3B on the third floor of this magnificent building, an historic event was about to take place. Mr J.H. Whitley, Chairman of the Board of Governors of the BBC, stood nervously in front of the microphone as the red 'on air' light winked twice and then stayed on. With that, the very first words of the new Empire Service were on the air – beamed from wintry London to the sunshine of Australia and New Zealand. Six days later it was known throughout the British Empire that a new instrument of almost unimaginable power had arrived. The power to bring together voices from countries across the world, a vital and tangible link across the Empire, was demonstrated admirably at 3pm on Christmas Day 1932, in a message spoken by King George V and broadcast from a temporary studio created at Sandringham.

The words, written by Rudyard Kipling, referred to the 'unifying force' of technology, and began as follows:

Through one of the marvels of modern science, I am enabled this Christmas Day to speak to all my peoples throughout the Empire. I take it as a good omen that wireless should have reached its present perfection at a time when the Empire has been linked in closer union, for it offers us immense possibilities to make that union closer still. It may be that our future will lay upon us more than one stern test. Our past will have taught us how to meet it unshaken. I speak to you now from my home and from my heart to you all, to men and women so cut off by the snows, the desert, or the sea that only voices out of the air can reach them.

As the sound of a global family sharing common interests, the broadcast made a huge impact on its Empire audience of twenty million. Few realised at the time that the global family would be drawn even closer by war just a few years hence.

In Germany in 1932 the Nazi Party came to power, and at the beginning of the following year Adolf Hitler became German Chancellor. In America in

PAST, PRESENT AND FUTURE

1932 President Roosevelt was elected to the first of his three terms of office in the White House, and on 1 January 1933 Japan attacked China in breach of a League of Nations agreement. The British Empire had interests in all these countries, and yet there seemed to be little appetite for, or concern expressed about, worldly issues. This was the era of Al Capone, the Loch Ness monster, the game Monopoly, Amelia Earhart, the era when air conditioning was invented and the Hindenburg airship crashed, when the helicopter was invented and the first demonstration of radar was given. This was when Rowntree created the Kit Kat and when Chamberlain announced 'Peace in our Time'. This was the 1930s, a decade that was riddled with contrast and paradox, the decade when the words 'streamlined' and 'glamorous' became fashionable and acceptable additions to the English language, and a decade when the English language itself was, thanks to the wireless, entering a new era of mass communication.

Doreen Price remembers Radio Normandie, which broadcast into the south of England:

> *We saw a poster in a shop window in Bournemouth, which was advertising Radio Normandie and its programmes. They were sponsored in those days. I know Victor Silvester was on one of the programmes because my mother loved his music. I know the children's programme was presented by the makers of something called 'Post Toasties'. Uncle Chris introduced it. When the war came, the station stopped broadcasting.*

Radio Normandie was on the air from 1926 to 1939. Programmes went out primarily on records, which were made in London. Some were broadcast live.

It was not just verbal communication that was increasing as the wireless started to reach the masses; visual communication in the form of films and newsreels was also entering a new phase. Films were shown at huge luxury cinemas such as the Rex, the Rialto, the Odeon and the Roxy, which were being built at the rate of three per week across the country. Cinemas were always full; anyone with style would want to be seen taking tea in a cinema restaurant, dolled up to the nines. Going to the cinema became part of a culture of escapism. This encompassed a new freedom of expression, something that the masses had experienced neither before nor during the First War, or through the Depression-hit years of the 1920s. This freedom was everywhere, including in music, where the new era of big swing bands, crooners and dances had begun. The prevailing mood seemed to be: 'Let's welcome the American take on life for today we are young and tomorrow, well, who knows what tomorrow will bring.'

In sedate Britain there were, perhaps inevitably, letters to the papers about the dangers of too much liberation for the masses, the evil that, for example, 'such wild dance' brought with it, even suggestions that it was the devil's dance. It was too new and too much for the old guard to accept. It was of course the old guard, the establishment, that controlled almost every aspect of life, including, not surprisingly, radio technology.

But listeners had little alternative than to tune in to the BBC and to its menu of fairly bland offerings, which were created by those in power who knew what was good for the audience. Granted, those offerings included some band music. A not untypical National Programme was that of Saturday, 21 August 1937. Henry Hall's Dance Orchestra was on the wireless at 12.30pm, followed by cricket. Later there was more organ music and forty minutes of Elsie Suddaby singing with Max Rostal on the violin. There were short stories, more orchestral music, talks on chastity, humility and obedience, news and weather, and a show featuring Jessie Matthews. This was called 'Past, Present and Future', and how apt that was at a very pivotal time in the nation's history.

Demand existed, however, for more popular music, especially for dance band music and hot jazz. To exploit this a private company, the International Broadcasting Company (IBC), was set up. It hired air time from overseas stations and transmitted popular programmes aimed at the British market from Radio Lyon, Radio Normandie, Radio Athlone, Radio Méditerranée and Radio Luxembourg. By 1938, Radio Luxembourg had 45 per cent of the Sunday listening audience against the BBC's 35 per cent. When war broke out, commercial broadcasting into Britain ceased, not least because Radio Luxembourg's transmitters fell into Nazi hands. Yet it was stations such as Luxembourg that first brought swing and big bands, and famous American names, to the British wireless listener; and their popularity grew. Margaret Semple, who lived near Dibden Purlieu, recalled:

> My dad, who was in a reserved occupation, played in a big band at the local's halls when the village or the local camp, organised dances. We had lemonade to drink and sandwiches to eat, and some very handsome young men to dance with. They were happy, simple, memorable occasions that helped take our minds off the war.

There were two types of big band at the peak of the genre's popularity. There were those known as 'sweet' bands, which were ballad heavy and more focused on melody; these were those heard on the BBC. The 'hot' bands were more rhythmically oriented and were more likely to appeal to fast swing dancers, such as those who did the jitterbug. When the Americans arrived in the New Forest, spearheaded by the USAAF, many local girls were literally swept off their feet by the high-rolling, smartly turned out 'Yanks' who could 'jitterbug at the drop of a dollar bill', as Pam Steele remembered:

> Several friends and me stayed in touch with some of the men, and we went dancing when the opportunity occurred, usually in Bournemouth and occasionally Stoney (Cross), but after D-Day we heard no more. In the 1990s, a large group of veterans returned to the Forest as part of a tour organised by Operation Friendly Invasion. I enquired about one of the chaps I used to go dancing with and they made enquiries in America, and sadly I learnt that he was killed on 27 July 1944. The war brought you together and then ripped you apart; well, emotionally it did anyway.

Operation Friendly Invasion stopped at Sopley Camp in Bransgore during its tour of Europe and the United Kingdom. Sopley was a site of mobile radar operations and is mentioned elsewhere in this book.

Now without commercial radio from Europe, the more gentle music was still being played by the traditional dance bands of Jack Hylton, Henry Hall,

These early post-war structures (built to the original wartime design) remain on the site of what was the radar station at Sopley. (Courtesy of Maxine Knott)

Women were employed on war work at Wellworthys Factory in Lymington. (Mary Evans Picture Library)

The original Second World War Garrison Theatre at Hurst Castle. (Maxine Knott)

The spirit of wartime entertainment lives on with occasional live shows at the Garrison Theatre, Hurst Castle. (Maxine Knott)

Percival Mackey, Ambrose and a whole host of others. Gradually, however, there was a marked shift towards the more popular swing, although this was, initially anyway, less strident than the sounds that had been coming from the American bands; sounds that audiences would eventually hear live when some of those bands played in theatres during the war years. Bill Percy, who travelled to the city from Lymington, said: 'When we were training in London we went to see the Savoy Orpheans. A live band was a great new experience for us, and I enjoyed that type of music right up until I lost my hearing about three years ago.'

The BBC regained its monopoly, and throughout the war years delivered, in accordance with the government's diktats, programmes such as 'Music While You Work', which was broadcast over factory loudspeaker systems and was aimed at boosting morale and keeping industry running, and 'Workers' Playtime', which was broadcast live from 'A factory canteen somewhere in Britain'.

Morale-boosting took on new heights through the use of music, song, dance and the cinema. Peggy Marshall from Bournemouth, at the edge of the New Forest, spoke of writing to her husband in the RAF:

We saw Gone with the Wind *before Jack left and we often quoted words from that film to each other in our many letters. It was our way of saying everything will be all right. When Jack was on leave, we used to try to visit the Gaumont for at least one of the dances there. They always had a live band and you could forget your troubles for a few hours.*

The wireless was to make a major contribution to the lives of men, women and children, and members of Britain's armed services at home and overseas, throughout the Second World War. Its positive impact was measured quite unscientifically by a doctor who transferred to Lymington Hospital in early 1944: 'People talk quite incessantly about wireless programmes and how they enjoy the escapism it gives them. They talk of band leaders and singers, comedy stars and stories as though they are personally involved with each. For some it seems a better tonic than I can prescribe. Thank goodness.'

WARTIME NEW FOREST REVEALED

2
The First Christmas

Nine-year-old evacuee Sidney Wallace was 'fostered' by a middle-aged couple living near Ringwood, together with two other younger children. A note that he wrote at the time included the heart-rending sentence 'Please Mr God, take me home to my Mummy. I hate it here.'

Evacuated from the Midlands on 31 August 1939, Sidney had not yet returned home, as many children had, in the previous couple of months of the so-called 'phoney war'. He was about to spend his very first Christmas away from home, away from his mother, Daphne, and his older sister, Betty, who had enlisted with the Red Cross. He was also separated from his younger sisters, Marion and Pauline, who had also been evacuated but were in Wiltshire. William, his father, had joined the Navy in 1937 and had been posted overseas.

Sidney knew that Christmas was not going to be the same as the wonderful ones he had enjoyed before. As much as he loved adventures, this was one he wanted to escape from. It was not anything like what he had expected or previously experienced: getting up at five o'clock every morning, helping his 'foster parents' with the other children, helping with the housework, including 'dirty' jobs such as cleaning the toilet and the scullery floor. There was little time for exploring the surrounding area or even playing with his fellow evacuees. Sidney was nothing more than an unpaid servant. This was very unfair, and he needed his mum more than anything. He had more questions than answers. Was this going to be the worst Christmas he had known in his young life? It felt odd, as though he was having a bad dream. Soon he hoped he would wake up, see his mum, then run towards her as fast as his little legs could manage, so she could give him the biggest cuddle ever.

Fortunately Sidney suffered no ill effects and was soon reunited with his mum. After the war he visited his former host family frequently from 1959 until 1990, when ill-health prevented him from doing so. Another aspect of evacuation troubled a local diarist. He pointed out that the majority of people were 'doing their share' by accepting evacuees willingly, but there were still a large number of big houses in the Forest that remained half empty. Wanting to stop what he saw as selfishness and waste, he also expressed concern that there were still people squandering huge sums on luxurious living while many others were unable to provide even minimal shelter and clothing for themselves. Yet those with money could, if they wished, spend it on helping the war effort. The local branches of the Salvation Army were amongst those calling for additional funds, in their case to purchase mobile canteens at a cost of £250 each and set up rest clubs for £1,250 each. Nationally, a million servicemen and women as well as civilians sought out the red shield sign every week, knowing that rest and refreshment would never be denied. Throughout the Forest, as the numbers of service personnel grew, the weight of demand upon the 'Sally Army' became heavier, not least upon the volunteers; yet they were there and always ready to serve.

Twenty-five-year-old Tom Clarke had joined the Grenadier Guards and spent his first Christmas on exercise in the New Forest. Common among his comrades, almost all of whom were new recruits and most of them younger than him, there was a feeling of resignation that Christmas 1939 was going to be a turning point. They knew from their fathers and grandfathers who had served in the First World War that 'Hope is good, but reality is what you get and nothing is ever the same again.' As much as they hoped the war would be over soon, they were facing up to the fact that there would be much death and destruction, and if they and their families survived, the world would be a vastly different place to the one they knew. So although Christmas was a welcome break, it was unlikely to distract them from what lay ahead.

Along the south coast of England, Trinity House vessels lay at anchor, helping to guide ships home for Christmas. A number of the lights had been mechanised, but for the crews on the other ships it was a precarious balance between keeping themselves safe from enemy attack, coping with the isolation and trying to enjoy

THE FIRST CHRISTMAS

From the top of Hurst Castle personnel would have seen the ships assembled for D-Day. (Maxine Knott)

Looking across the Solent from Hurst Castle on a stormy day. (Maxine Knott)

isolation and trying to enjoy a Christmas at sea away from their loved ones. The lightshipmen were regarded by the popular press as symbols of a burning hope, and beacons of an undarkened faith. 'In carrying on their lonely task, they are preserving for the rest of us, the very spirit of the Christmas season,' wrote one journalist.

Another journalist, meanwhile, had visited Lyndhurst, where a woman complained that since everyone was fighting for their very existence, there was no justification for a Christmas break for munitions workers. No one denied that production during every hour of every day was of vital importance, but her concern was that workers desiring holidays were showing a fundamental inability to grasp the gravity of the situation!

In his Christmas sermon, the Archbishop of York was to reflect the mood of the nation well; its desire for guidance, reassurance and hope. Listeners across the New Forest huddled around their wirelesses, listening thoughtfully as the words resonated with their own feelings; Christmas, usually a time of joy, was now a time of disbelief and anxiety. The archbishop spoke about the dangers of escaping from reality, the need for moral revolution and what could be done to comfort each other.

This sermon, many noted, was 'Churchillian' in nature: inspiring yet realistic; a morale-boosting effort that went some way towards encouraging everyone to be positive.

One of the many written legacies of the wartime Forest was attributed to Sally Parnell, who in 1939 was a social commentator producing reports for the national press. She wrote, from her home near Hythe:

> *A season of change, ahead of a New Year,*
> *The people change, now full of fear,*
> *Unknown the future and what it will bring,*
> *To the glory of God we must all sing,*
> *This peaceful place, A forest of calm,*
> *Now full of uncertainty, worry and alarm,*
> *For if this war is as bad as the last,*
> *For certain the fateful dye has been cast.*

Among the many rumours that the population had to contend with in the days leading up to the first wartime Christmas was the belief that married women and widows would be asked to surrender their wedding rings to help the government pay for the war. The rumour circulated again a year later, most likely prompted by the fact that in Italy under Mussolini women were indeed required to give up jewellery and rings.

As depleted families around the country sat down at the table, as those evacuees and the hundreds of orphaned children from Europe spent their first Christmas with strangers, and as the men and women who had been called up for duty in civilian roles and for service in the Forces lined up in the canteens, sat in makeshift shelters or joined their hosts, the spirit and meaning of the season brought them together. For one day, the nation was as one. As a diarist recorded for a radio programme that was broadcast after the war, 'We knew then that whatever was to come, we would give of our best, we would strive to win through and we would overcome the challenges for the sake of our children and the survival of our country and the free world.'

King George VI was not a competent speaker, yet through his Christmas broadcast he succeeded in galvanising his people, He ended his speech with a quote from a poem written in 1908 by Minnie Louise Haskins:

I said to the man who stood at the Gate of the Year,
Give me a light that I may tread safely into the unknown.
And he replied:
"Go out into the darkness, and put your hand into the Hand of God.
That shall be better than light, and safer than a known way."

In stark contrast to this, across the North Sea the population of Germany had by Christmas 1939 already been subjected to six years of propaganda, which had led them to believe that the country was mighty and just in bringing war to Europe. The message was all about uniting German people in a righteous cause; yet when blackouts, rationing and winter relief campaigns became compulsory, privately and in hushed circles many started questioning the cause they were supporting. At Christmas, there was *Eintopf*, which was described by American correspondent William Shirer thus: '*Eintopf*, a one-pot meal which means all you can get for lunch is a cheap stew. But you pay the price of a big meal for it, the difference going to the winter relief, or so they say. Actually, it goes into the war chest.'

German girls had already had a taste of things to come through membership of the Bund Deutscher Madel (BDM), the League of German Maidens. They reported for duty on the Home Front, and by that first Christmas of the war their indoctrination was well under way. They lost their individuality in order to become wholly hardened, their simple identical dress and enforced lack of makeup helping to further the eradication of personal thought and deed. The Hitler Youth movement was helping to spread anti-Semitism and was also recruiting new members, as were the armed services, especially the SS. The Schutzstaffel, or Protective Echelon, the black-uniformed elite corps of the

Nazi Party, had been founded by Adolf Hitler in April 1925 as a small personal bodyguard, but had grown with the success of the Nazi movement and, gathering immense police and military powers, had become virtually a state within a state. Over half a million people, mostly the young, the sick and the infirm, had been evacuated into the countryside, and they would spend that first Christmas away from their loved ones. Swastika flags were everywhere, and many homes used them instead of traditional decorations. Set against the bleakness of life for the majority, and the controlled society, the Nazi machine was working flat out even on Christmas Eve just to reinforce its message and the expectations it had of its people. Berlin's *Morgenpost* (Morning Post) ran an article headlined 'Rudolf Hess addresses an unmarried mother':

> *As all National Socialists know, the highest law in war as in peace is as follows; preservation of the Race. Every custom, law and opinion has to give way and adapt itself to this highest law. Such an unmarried mother may have a hard path, but she knows that when we are at war it is better to have a child under the most difficult conditions than not to have one at all. It is taken for granted today that a woman and mother who are widowed or divorced may marry again. It must also be taken for granted that a woman who has a war child may enter into marriage with a man who is not the father of that child. A race, especially during war, cannot afford to neglect to keep and continue its national heritage. The highest duty a woman can perform is to bear racially healthy children. Be happy good woman that you have been permitted to perform this highest duty for Germany.*

Around the New Forest as elsewhere in Britain, people tucked into the first wartime Christmas dinner. Jess Walker of Holbury recalled toasting absent friends, a swift end to the war and a better tomorrow:

> *Many of us were trying out one of the many new recipes using rationed goods and a great deal of imagination. It was for our generation a strange almost unreal contrast between celebrating Christmas and*

knowing that we were at war, and the suffering was just beginning. We went out for a walk later in the day and stood for a while taking in the Forest landscape and we wondered if all this would be lost. Fortunately, it was to be lost to our own army for the duration of the war rather than to an occupying enemy, so there is hope in life.

And so it was Christmas in spite of everything, in spite of it all.

3
THE TIDE OF WAR

Having thus far set the scene and reflected on the state of the nation and the world, and the initial effects of war on the New Forest and its impact on local communities, we have the foundations upon which to build the next phase of the story.

Specifically, whilst we have formed an idea about how the war was to physically affect the Forest and its people, we can also begin to understand the extent of the social and environmental changes. It is these latter which have left us with a tangible legacy of those far off and desperate days; days that will soon no longer be within living memory. Whilst remains of the built environment are evidence of the core role of the area during its occupation by Allied armed services during the war years, it is vital that we continue to record and document the all too easily lost social legacy. Every snippet of information and every faded photograph, every anecdote and every memory will have a place in history when those for whom the war was a personal experience pass, and when our ability to touch our heritage will be immeasurably diminished. We will be even more reliant upon written testimony, testimony that tells us of the reality of lives lived: the rationing, blackouts, make do and mend, war funds weeks, evacuees, queuing, knitting for the troops, rules and regulations including compulsory carrying of gas masks, recycling and tending to allotments. Many records speak of helping each other, camaraderie, walking miles to visit family and friends, visits to the cinema, comforting the bereaved and missing their brothers, husbands, fathers and lovers.

Anecdotes about the initial influx of evacuees in 1939 overwhelming the Women's Institute (WI) at Milford on Sea contrast with stories of 'strange goings

Ready to defend to the last man: members of a typical Home Guard Unit. (Phil Simmonds)

on' in Sway, which were eventually revealed as being night training exercises by the Home Guard. They speak as well of one of the air raids on New Milton, which killed nineteen civilians and a number of servicemen. Jim Gould vividly remembers the horror of seeing a car on fire at the crossroads in the centre of the town, with the occupant being consumed by the flames. The fierce fire prevented any attempts at rescuing the driver. Jim was 'frozen on the spot, stunned at what I was seeing'. Another witness, Jude James, says that there was a controlled panic:

> *The war had come to us and although we had been preparing for it, the suddenness and ferocity of the attack against the town caused some people to run, others simply to rush forward to see what, if anything they could do to help. There was a lot of screaming. As a youngster that upset me a great deal.*

Official documents prepared ahead of the war by the Emergency Planning Committee were part of the planning for incidents like this: 'It was reported that there were 7800 spaces available in cemeteries throughout the district. Subject to certain agreed rules and regulations, some ten churches in the area were prepared to permit the use of their buildings as temporary mortuaries.'

There is also anecdotal record of enemy aircraft strafing New Milton's

The Hinton Admiral (Christchurch) pillbox, which was positioned to guard the railway line. (NFNPA)

Dorothy's Café opened in 1940, and is still owned by the same family. (Maxine Knott)

Evacuees enjoy the local countryside – a scene recreated by Nick Halling. (Nick Halling)

railway line, station and bridge, with young children who had been trainspotting scrambling for cover. Just a few steps north of that railway bridge is Dorothy's Café, which opened in 1940 and very quickly became a meeting place for locals, airmen from Lymington and Holmsley airfields and many service personnel who were in transit. Noted for both its home-cooked food and its home-from-home atmosphere, it remains in the ownership of the same family to this day, and is a tangible social legacy of the wartime era.

So too is the Memorial Hall in Whitefield Road, which is the successor to a building that was erected on the site in 1930. The land was purchased by the post-First World War Brotherhood from Milton Unionist Club (Conservative Club) by a conveyance dated 31 December 1929. The Public Hall, as it was then known, must have run into difficulties during the Second World War because eventually, in February 1943, it was let to the local firm Moody Son & Co. as a furniture repository. With the coming of peace in May 1945, the people of New Milton cast about for a suitable memorial to all the men and women from that part of Hampshire who had lost their lives, and the *Lymington Times* dated 1 September 1945 published the first list of donations for the purchase of the hall as that memorial. It was to be used as the British Legion local headquarters and as a community centre for the town. The Trust deed said that if the Legion could not continue the successful management of the Hall, it was to call a public meeting for residents to decide its future. And so, in 1945, the War Memorial Hall started its new life, and it remains today as a symbol of remembrance.

Records tell of schools that were evacuated to safe areas. For example, Portsmouth Grammar School in Hampshire relocated to Brockenhurst School. Vera Wallis of Ringwood remembered: 'Where evacuees increased local school populations, classes were often taken on a half-day basis. Half-a-day's schooling for local children in the morning, with evacuees being taught in the afternoon, for example.'

Local people who opened their homes to the evacuees were paid the sum of 10s 6d per week (about £15 today), although this was reduced to 8s 6d (about £12 today) per child if two or more children were billeted at the same address.

In some areas, teachers from evacuated towns and cities were drafted in to help with the additional workload placed on small country schools. For evacuees, it was reassuring to have someone from their own community, for example their own teacher, with them.

Some former evacuees, such as Joan Coup who retired to New Milton, report that they enjoyed their time making friends with the local kids, and that evacuation taught them confidence and skills that they used in later life.

Children walked or cycled everywhere, but even their personal mobility was affected fundamentally by the war – as security became a primary concern. For adults, of course, matters were much worse. John (now Lord) Teynham, remembers being stopped at the gated entrance to the cottage where he then lived, near an airfield: 'A huge giant of an American GI checked my ID card every time I left and returned to the cottage.' In addition, many private vehicles were taken off the road because owners were not entitled to petrol coupons. A number of cars, lorries and vans were requisitioned by various government departments, local authorities and the emergency services, so they could fulfil their vastly increased duties. There were exemptions, including vehicles used by doctors and members of the Women's Voluntary Service. Petrol was also available for farmers and those engaged in other vital work for the war effort. Betty Hockey, who ran the Non-Stops Concert Party, which toured various military camps around the Forest, was able to secure enough fuel to meet all their performance commitments:

> It was considered we were keeping up the morale of the servicemen and women and so we never really had problems about getting fuel. Later in the war when the Americans arrived, they gave us all the fuel we needed. Well after all, we were entertaining a lot of GIs by then.

GI means General Issue, and was stamped on much US equipment. It was the nickname given to American soldiers.

Car sharing was popular, as was hitch-hiking, which according to some records peaked in 1943 and 1945. To get around the problem of petrol rationing, people came up with alternative methods of power, including gas stored on the roof of vehicles in large sealed bags. The bicycle became the main form of transport, although walking was for many the obvious way of getting around.

> Telephone: Beaulieu 318.
>
> **VERDERERS, NEW FOREST.**
>
> From HUBERT FORWARD, Agister, Beaulieu, Brockenhurst.
>
> 28th Dec 1943
>
> Dear Sir,
>
> I beg to report that the Royal Navy are carrying out some sort of work on the south side of Hatchet Pond. Also a trench has been dug across the open forest from Furzy Lodge to Pinnerley Bridge and a water pipe line is being laid. And near Pinnerley House, Beaulieu, a large Hut has been erected by the Army on the open forest on a piece of very good pasture.
>
> I am Sir
> Your Obediently
> Hubert Forward Agister
>
> Mr Chandler Esq
> Romsey.

Every activity was reported back to the authorities. (Author's collection)

The Redbridge pillbox, close to Totton, along the main railway line to Southampton. (NFNPA)

Even the road system itself was affected. According to the records of the Forest's Verderers' Court: 'Ahead of D-Day nearly 25 miles of road were widened an average of 4 feet and this effectively removed from general use 25 acres of Forest land.'

Train travel was severely restricted during the early years of the war, with armed services personnel being given priority. Later, during the build-up to D-Day in 1944, further restrictions were placed on the railways. Posters were used as part of a massive propaganda campaign to ask 'Is your journey really necessary', and encourage passengers to 'give your place to a member of the fighting services'.

Lilian Maxwell, formerly of Bransgore, remembered that these posters related to transport were just a few of thousands that were displayed, covering subjects such as gardening, the enemy, collecting for ships and aircraft, knitting for the troops, health and make do and mend:

You have to remember that the wartime generation was very susceptible to such campaigns and we never questioned the messages and instructions that we were given. Even adverts in newspapers and magazines for items such as toothpaste and shoe polish had either a slogan or an image that linked them to the war effort.

Cinemas and the wireless were also pivotal in the success of the propaganda campaign, and there was a whole genre of wartime films, many made in America, that were scripted and filmed in such a way as to boost the morale and lift the spirit of the people. *Mrs Miniver, Went the Day Well?* and *A Canterbury Tale* were amongst the greatest of all patriotic flag-waving films, which were screened in cinemas such as the Regal in Ringwood (still standing, but boarded up), the Waverley in New Milton (long gone), the Lyric in Lymington (now a shop) and the Regent in Christchurch, now a thriving arts centre and cinema. These and many other local cinemas, most since demolished, welcomed Americans from local Forest airfields and service personnel from many Allied countries.

In contrast to these memories, which will fade unless recorded, remains of the wartime built environment, such as pillboxes and pieces of concrete

A supermarket now stands on the site of the former Lyric Cinema in the High Street, Lymington, which in essence has changed very little. (Frank Tillyer)

runway, hard-standings and so-called temporary buildings, will, through the efforts of the New Forest National Park Authority and the myriad of history and preservation groups in the area, continue for many years to provoke thoughts about and promote consideration of the many thousands of men, women and children for whom the Forest was home during the Second World War. Sometimes, written records refer to structures that we can still observe – as in this extract from a post-war diary: 'Eling Tide Mill, near Totton, supplied water to the nearby Agwi [Fawley] refinery, which in turn supplied fuel via the Pipe Line Under the Ocean [PLUTO] to the shores of France. Eight Marines were assigned the task of guarding Eling, although they all complained that they wanted to see more action than that location could ever provide.'

Memories of wartime are also inspired by the memorials that have been erected by local organisations and authorities across the Forest to

The remains of many wartime structures are on private land, and access should not be attempted without the landowner's permission. (NFNPA)

Veterans took part in annual ceremonies at Lepe Country Park. (Author's collection)

D-Day veteran Ron Walsh RN at Lepe during a commemoration. (Author's collection)

For a number of years an annual ceremony of commemoration was held on the beach at Lepe. (Author's collection)

commemorate the personnel who served and their legacy. Standing by one memorial, set some 50ft above a beach, watching the waves gently folding back on themselves as they hit the pebbled shore, it is very hard to imagine that today's calm scene correlates in any way with those desperate days when men and machines were prepared for what was curiously called by some commentators 'The Great Adventure'. We are at a place called Lepe (pronounced leap), or more specifically Lepe Country Park, which for many visitors to the area will be the first window on the wartime history of the New Forest. Lepe is at the end of Southampton Water, overlooking the Isle of Wight, with Bournemouth Bay to the west and Portsmouth to the east. If anyone wants to know where this hamlet is, most of those offering directions will probably say 'It's near Beaulieu.' Well, yes it is, and it is not far from Exbury House and Gardens either.

    Here you can discover the stories of PLUTO. Operation Pluto was a joint operation between British engineers, oil companies and armed forces to construct oil pipelines under the English Channel between England and France in support of Operation Overlord. The scheme was developed by Arthur Hartley, chief engineer with the Anglo-Iranian Oil Company. You can also find out about the Mulberry Harbour, the Women's Royal Naval Service (WRENs), which operated small craft on stormy days, and Operation Neptune, which was the cross-Channel phase of Operation Overlord. Operation Neptune placed all naval issues under the command of Admiral Bertram Ramsey, whose command skill had already been seen in 1940 when he played a vital part in the evacuation of troops from Dunkirk. During the build-up to D-Day, columns of Sherman tanks were parked under the pine trees here. The Sowley boom anti-submarine net was strung out under the sea from a position close to the beach. It was only recently removed, because it was deemed a hazard to shipping. For such a small area it made such a huge contribution to the war effort; it is just overflowing with history. When you visit Lepe, you can enjoy the very useful audio tours, or if you prefer, explore, take photographs, then go away and read the reference books. Perhaps you will be able to find someone who can talk first hand about the place, for there are still those who, like Tom Charlton, were youngsters during the war:

Landing craft moored in the Solent off Lepe Beach. (Author's collection)

Remains of Mulberry Harbour construction can still be seen on the shore at Lepe. (Author's collection)

We weren't evacuated during the war because we lived in a so-called safe area in the Forest and we could get on our bikes and ride around although when it got to spring of 1944, things started to change and a lot of roads were closed and areas shut off to the public. We came down to Lepe a few times and it was exciting seeing all the activity. We thought it was just another military camp and it wasn't until after D-Day was it clear how important it was. After the war we came and played on the site and there was still a lot of concrete and a lot of discarded material.

Flying over the site provides an enhanced view of the footprints of buildings and concrete emplacements, including the remains of Mulberry construction, can still be seen quite clearly. At ground level, which most visitors will enjoy, it's more of a hands on history experience. This area, integral to the massive build-up for D-Day, was destined for a place in the history books, not least because of its prime position right on the Solent.

Alison Steele, former Park Manager, spoke about the area:

We look out across to the Island and to your right you can see the red and green posts marking the entrance to the River Beaulieu. During the war, the whole of this river estuary was requisitioned by the Navy, and there would be a constant stream of military craft going past Lepe rather than the recreational boats we can see today. A lot of the larger craft would have been stood offshore here. Smaller craft would be plying to and fro. Many of those would have been manned by WRENs who were based at nearby Beaulieu. They had to be out in all weathers; believe me, a strong south-westerly wind whistling up the Solent can produce some big waves. They had to go out sometimes at night-time, ferrying equipment out to the larger vessels and perhaps occasionally taking the odd drunken sailor back home. Just a little further along the estuary of the River Beaulieu is Lepe House, which is one of the eleven large houses that were requisitioned locally for use by military personnel during the war. Its position here at the entrance to the river Beaulieu

A Liberty Ship at anchor in the Solent. (Author's collection)

> made it an important signals base for naval activities. Along the beach, if you were to go further you would come to Inchmery House and that was a base for training Polish and French troops.

Mention must be made again of one of the key facts about this area. Depending on which source you quote from, between 6,000 and 9,000 American troops left from Lepe for Operation Overlord, and therefore it is right that the focal point of this country park is the magnificent memorial. A visitor, Royal Army Service Corps (RASC) veteran Fred Nicholas, commented that he found the memorial 'very moving':

> They have gone to a lot of trouble to acknowledge what our generation went through. It brought back a lot of memories for me, some sad, some happy. I was very impressed with what I saw, and I think it's good that the public still remember for the sake of all the lads that didn't come home.

4

WATCHING AND WAITING

The role of the New Forest, specifically during the Second World War, cannot be viewed in isolation from events, developments and emergency planning which involved and affected the wider county, and indeed the country as a whole. The Forest's pivotal contribution to the D-Day campaign was made possible not just by its location, its geographical features and its valuable natural assets, but also by the addition of expertise and specialist skills from many areas. Here is the story of one such contribution, which does not receive a great deal of historical acknowledgement yet at the time played a major role throughout the New Forest and has left visible footprints in the history and fabric of the area.

The story begins in the Weald of Kent, some 15 miles south of Maidstone, in the small town of Cranbrook, with its solid square-towered church of weathered stone and its nineteenth-century windmill. Here it was that in 1924 Major General Ashmore and the Chief Constable of Kent set up an observation post to track the course of aircraft and to report on them. There were eight similar observation posts at other sites in Kent, and they were all linked by telephone to the exchange in Cranbrook Post Office – where an upstairs room became known as the 'Centre'.

Major General Ashmore CB, CMGV, MVO had been put in charge of the defences of London as far back as the autumn of 1917, and he subsequently created the London Air Defence Area (LADA). This organisation coordinated reports from coastal and inland watching posts, searchlights, gun stations, balloons and aerodromes to the south and south-east of London, yet following the end of the First World War, the authorities lost interest in the project.

The RAF, which was the most powerful service of its type in the world with 20,000 aircraft, had by March 1923 a mere three squadrons allocated to home defence. Not surprisingly it was Winston Churchill who insisted on keeping alive the intricate and specialised art of air defence. As a result of pressure by Churchill and a Committee of Inquiry report, it was agreed that 'a highly-organised system is essential for the rapid collection and distribution of information and intelligence regarding the movements of hostile and friendly aircraft throughout the whole area of possible air operations'.

Following the success of the trials that involved the Cranbrook Centre and its other eight posts, it was decided to extend the system to twenty-seven posts in Kent and sixteen in Sussex, with centres in Maidstone and Horsham respectively.

In the summer of 1925 three squadrons of aircraft participated in complex simulated attacks on the capital. All were successfully tracked and plotted. The report of the trials was accepted, and on 29 October 1925 its recommendations were put into effect, making the Observer Corps (OC) an official organisation.

Following the formation of No. 1 Group in Kent and No. 2 Group in Sussex, Major General Ashmore turned his attention to the county of Hampshire, which he surveyed in the early months of 1926. Home defence was the responsibility of the War Office, which delegated local control to the chief constable of each county. It was from the ranks of special constables that the nucleus of the teams who worked in the Cranbrook Centre and at the Observation Posts (OPs) in the field, were selected. Locally, as more members were recruited, so they too became special constables, and by May 1926 Brigadier General Du Boulay CMG had been chosen as Winchester's first Controller, and a small room was provided in Winchester's post office as Hampshire's Centre.

On 1 June 1926, Major General Ashmore met his new Controller, the Chief Constable of Hampshire and some of the OC Specials at the post office in Winchester, to explain the new reporting system. No. 3 Group was created, and by the end of 1926 there were twenty-three observation and reporting sites in the county. They were linked by telephone in clusters of three to the Centre in Winchester, but soon space in the tiny room at the post office became a problem. In 1927, the Centre and its switchboard moved to a bigger room in a nearby store and here it remained until 1933, when it transferred to the Blue Triangle Club in Winchester, which was also the Young Women's Christian Association (YWCA) headquarters.

General Du Boulay retired in 1933 and was succeeded by Colonel G.N. Salmon CMG, DSO. During his first two years, clusters of posts were added to the map, including coverage of the Isle of Wight, where posts were established at Newport, Sandown, Niton and Freshwater.

On 1 January 1929, control of the OC had been transferred from the War Office to the Air Ministry, which had now became responsible for training, although chief constables were still in charge of recruiting and controlling personnel. On 8 March 1929, the Air Ministry appointed Air Commodore G.A.D. Masterman as its first commandant.

Meanwhile, Centre personnel in their room at the YWCA in Winchester had been complaining for some time that dance music from the Blue Triangle Club in the same building was interfering with their duties, and so the Centre was moved once more, this time to a wooden building erected on the roof of the Post Office Telephone Exchange in Brook Street. It was from this exposed and vulnerable position that they participated in the August 1939 air exercises, and a month later listened to Chamberlain's announcement on 3 September that this country was at war with Germany. Just as exposed, if not more so, were the observers in the field, who were equipped with no more than a canvas screen to keep some of the draught from their legs. At the outbreak of war, each post was allowed to spend £5 to build a protective structure, and many weird and wonderful creations resulted. Lockerley Green Post boasted a plumber, a builder and a coal merchant among their number, and they built a splendid home from home with rotating windscreens and central heating – a far cry from the bare field and its solitary telegraph pole that they started with in 1926! Tracking by sound had been practised successfully from the early days. At no. 3/G2 Post located in Sway, the Head Observer was First World War veteran Engineer Captain R.H.C. Ball. He took part in official plotting trials with a Vickers Virginia aircraft from RAF Worthy Down. Captain Ball is also credited with the design of the standard post plotting instrument for which a Royal Observer Corps (ROC) observer named Micklethwait later designed the height corrector.

The Winchester OC Centre moved out of its dangerous location on the Post Office roof in 1940 and took up residence in Northgate House in Jewry Street. Here it was to remain throughout the Battle of Britain and the busy two years following, before moving finally in 1943 to a purpose-built Operations Centre in Abbotts Road on the city outskirts. Colonel Salmon, the Controller, had been joined in 1938 by Major General Sir William Twiss KCIE, CB, CBE, MC, as Observer Group Officer, and it was he who took over as Winchester's first Group Commandant in 1943 when Colonel Salmon retired.

The Winchester Group was privileged to contribute to the development of a number of plotting and reporting techniques, not least of which was assistance to friendly aircraft lost or in distress, a story told by Wing Commander Bulmore in his book *The Dark Haven*. In 1943, further aircraft reporting posts were added to the Group, which now covered not only Hampshire, the New Forest and the Isle of Wight, but also the fringes of Sussex, Surrey, Oxfordshire, Wiltshire and Dorset in a network of some eighty posts linked in clusters of threes and fours by telephone to the Centre in Winchester. It was the time of the enemy hit-and-run raider, individual pilots who flew at low level using valleys and natural features to avoid detection. The ROC rose to the challenge and introduced fast tracking methods.

During 1943 and the early part of 1944, through what was the start of the build-up to D-Day, Hampshire and the New Forest were in the thick of it, so much so that the 'mass plot' was introduced for occasions when large formations or constant streams too numerous to be counted passed over. The ROC was quite appropriately referred to as 'the eyes and ears of the RAF' because throughout the war they identified and tracked all aircraft flying over the country by day and by night. Radar beams were directed seaward to provide advance information of incoming flights, and once these aircraft could be seen from the coast they were 'handed over' to the ROC for further tracking. Information from the posts was collated at their Centres and passed to Fighter Command, which directed fighters to intercept the incoming enemy fighters and bombers, and passed information on to the Air Raid warning network and other interested parties. All of the raids during the Battle of Britain, the London Blitz and the big air raids on cities such as Coventry were handled in this way.

The Battle of Britain is so well documented that the details will not be repeated here. Suffice to say that the OC was justifiably proud of the part it played in the battle, and official recognition came on 9 April 1941, when it was announced in Parliament that 'in recognition of the valuable services rendered by the Observer Corps over a number of years, His Majesty the King has been graciously pleased to approve that the Corps shall henceforth be known by the style and description of The Royal Observer Corps'.

The amphibious landings at Dieppe on 19 August 1942, although a disaster, highlighted a number of lessons to be learnt, one of which was that many Allied planes were being shot down by our own gunners. This prompted Air Vice Marshal Sir Trafford Leigh-Mallory KCB, DSO, RAF, then commanding 11 Group, to suggest that naval gunners should be trained in aircraft recognition. He went on to suggest that ROC personnel would be suitable for this task. Although the use of the ROC was rejected by the Air Ministry, the need for men skilled in aircraft recognition to be carried on ships was recognised. Subsequent losses of Allied planes from friendly fire generally, and specifically at the landings at Salerno and Sicily, only served to emphasise the need.

As planning for the invasion of occupied Europe got under way, it became apparent that the aircraft recognition experts already in the Services, RAF aircrew and certain anti-aircraft units in the Army, were going to be otherwise engaged. Air Chief Marshal Leigh-Mallory's suggestion of employing members of the ROC as aircraft identifiers was therefore resurrected and subsequently adopted. Thus what was known as the Seaborne project, whereby members of the Royal Observer Corps took part in the invasion of Europe, came about. While the 'Seabornes' were away, the first V1 flying bombs were sighted (13 June 1944), and they continued to rain down until 29 March 1945, when their launch sites in France and Holland were overrun. Almost all were targeted on London. To meet this new threat, some Observers were drafted to help man the posts in and around London. Once again, the Corps played a considerable and mostly unsung part in the defeat of the V1s. They were less effective against the V2s, but then the entire defence system was seemingly powerless against them. More than 1,000 were plotted between 8 September 1944 and 27 March 1945, and their sites of impact were reported.

Watching and waiting for nightly raids became something of a routine for many. (Wayne Johnson)

A re-enactor depicts a member of the wartime Observer Corps. (Nick Halling)

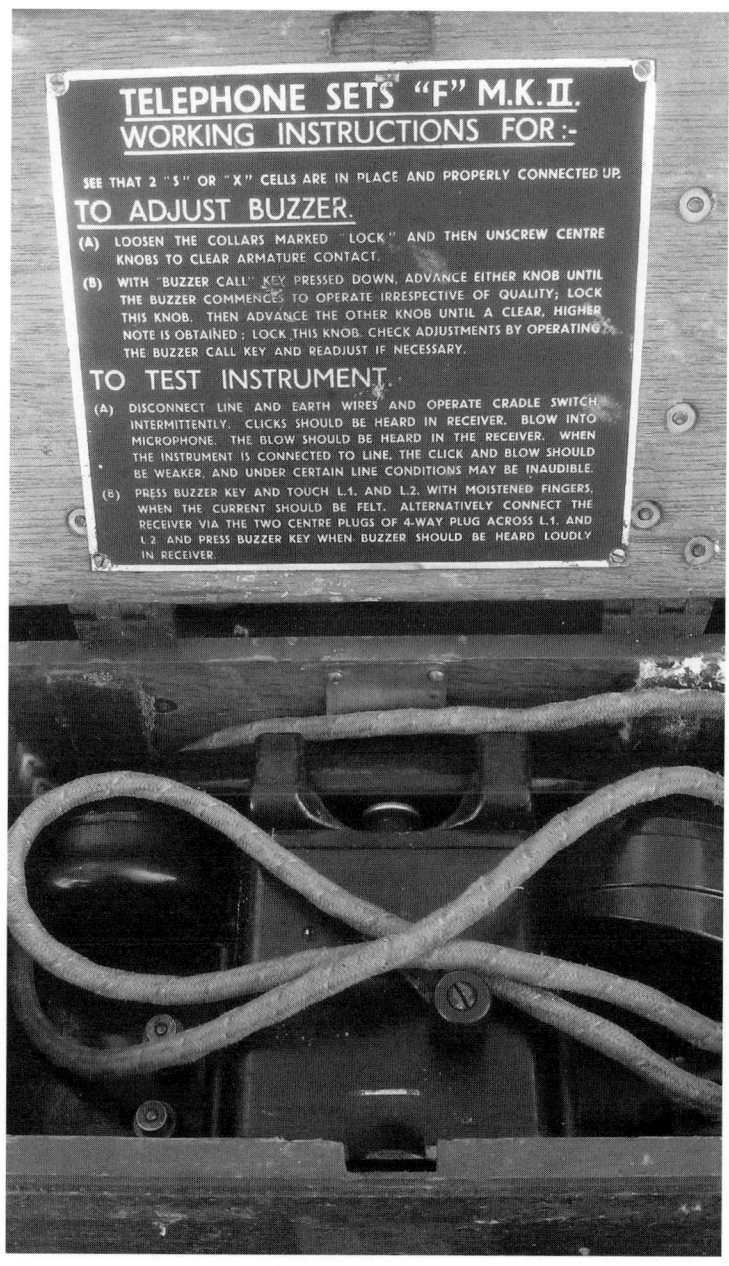

This field telephone was of the type used in Observation Points. (Author's collection)

Forward Aircraft Observation Posts were built at the following locations in the New Forest:

- Barton (Specialist Satellite Post or SSP)
- Christchurch and Copythorne (this site is buried beneath the M27 motorway)
- Exbury
- Fordingbridge
- Hengistbury (SSP)
- Keyhaven (SSP)
- Lyndhurst
- Marchwood
- New Milton
- Ringwood
- Sway
- Verwood

Evidence of some of these sites is still visible, but it is important to check with the ROC Museum (see reference section). The role they played was one of vital support, particularly during 1943 and in the months up to and including D-Day.

By the spring of 1945 the end of the war was finally in sight. German air raids were sporadic and were generally restricted to low-level hit-and-run attacks on airfields and the like, and some reconnaissance flights were being made by the enemy's new Arado 234B jets. The ROC was stood down on 12 May 1945, just four days after Victory in Europe (VE) Day. There was much clearing up to be done at this stage and a number of end-of-war parades to take part in, but of course the full-time men and women were now out of a job. The 1945 Birthday Honours List and the 1946 New Year Honours List contained sixty names which were awarded a total of four OBEs (Order of the British Empire), fourteen MBEs (Member of the Order of the British Empire) and forty-two BEMs (British Empire Medal) in final recognition of the war service of the ROC.

A small cadre of officers was maintained at ROC Headquarters and caretaker officers were appointed to every Group and Area. It was soon realised that there would be a peacetime role for the ROC, and after eighteen months in limbo the call went out for the Corps to recommence training.

5
Hands Across The Sea

Often described in past times as the 'Threshold of Ocean and Empire', the port of Southampton continues to play its part in the life of the nation, both in times of peace and of war. Its role during the Second World War in particular is well documented. On the north-western outskirts of the city is a community that played its part in the war effort, and whilst not on the front line in the same way as its neighbour, Totton hosted a vital service that helped to fight the war on the Home Front.

An early twentieth-century traveller wrote:

Beyond Totton for the first miles, a stranger may be forgiven both impatience and the question, 'Where is the Forest?', but gradually the orderly ordinariness of the road grows less, and after the railway is crossed at Lyndhurst Road [now known as Ashurst Station; there is a Second World War shelter nearby] one might be passing through a very spacious and somewhat unkempt park, yet this is the Forest.

Totton is indeed on the cusp of the Forest, and is clustered around the main arterial routes into the area: from Southampton (the A33), from Salisbury (the A326) and the M27 motorway junction. The A36 takes the visitor through the town centre. Testwood Lane leads to Testwood Sports College, a relatively new name for Testwood School, which opened on this site in 1946. Take a moment to observe the older parts of the school and its obvious pre-war utilitarian style.

The building at Testwood was requisitioned by the government and pressed into service for the war effort. It became a regional training centre for National

Fire Service (NFS) personnel, and in 1942, under the auspices of the NFS, it welcomed men of the Canadian Corps of Fire Fighters (also known as the Civilian Corps of Canadian Fire Fighters), who were volunteers drawn from military and civilian fire brigades throughout Canada.

The little-known story of the 406 firemen who served in England between 1942 and 1945 is as fascinating as it is inspiring. Having given up their safe existence in Canada to travel through U-boat-infested waters to an uncertain future helping fight fires on the Home Front, these volunteers excelled in their duties and left a lasting impression on all those with whom they served and met during their time in England.

Just two years from its mobilisation in September 1939, the peacetime Fire Service had, despite many operational problems and other related difficulties, met the challenges thrust upon it by war. The peacetime strength of some 50,000 personnel had expanded, in its new civil defence role, from 200,000 at the outbreak of war to about 300,000 by the spring of 1941. The core strength comprised regular firemen, volunteers, part-timers and members of the Auxiliary Fire Service. In addition, there were stirrup parties, as well as various supplementary fire-fighting groups, including those employed by private estates in the New Forest.

However, there was a need for more help. Bombing of English cities continued, and although there was a brief lull, in mid-1941 further significant attacks took place on London. The Fire Service had now been nationalised. A renewed call for assistance went out from the British government, and further consideration was given to the formation of a Canadian fire-fighting unit to serve in the United Kingdom.

Various meetings took place between and within the British and Canadian governments, when matters including pay, pension, benefits, transportation, recruitment, finance and equipment for, and the actual status of, the firefighters were discussed at length. From 24 June 1942 and for several months thereafter, a total of 406 volunteers in several contingents arrived in the United Kingdom, and after training and familiarisation at Testwood (and Ivybridge in Devon), units were posted to major cities including London, Southampton and Portsmouth.

Canadian firefighters who were trained in Totton helped to carry out trials of PLUTO at Lepe Beach. (Author's collection)

The late Cyril Kendall of Totton was an officer in the NFS: 'The Canadians donated thousands of feet of rubber hose which became known, not surprisingly as Canadian Hose. That was one of the best things that ever happened, getting all that hose which fitted, and with the addition of our connectors could be used anywhere.'

Jack Coulter served with the Corps of Canadian Fire Fighters. During his time in the Corps, he became a Leading Fire Fighter.

> We arrived in Liverpool after nine days at sea. Our ship, the Dominion Monarch, had been part-converted into a troop ship. I lived on bread and cheese and jam for the entire journey. The mutton they offered me was not edible.
>
> Immediately upon arrival, we were put on a train for Southampton, and from there we were transported to Testwood, just outside the city in a district called Totton. The grounds had been converted into a

May Belbin, second from right, with Canadian firefighters at Totton, c.1943. (Author's collection)

National Fire Service catering teams served hundreds of meals every day. (NFRS)

training facility for the National Fire Service.

We learnt real quick the techniques of the different trailer pumps and hydrants, and the fact that air raids often destroyed the water mains. In the city, there were large steel and concrete tanks full of water, and in some cases, basements of buildings were used for water storage.

We were often called to travel to other locations and one time we went to Bournemouth where we spent two weeks after one raid.

Home for us was the Alliance Hotel in Southampton.

Detachment 1 was sent to Southampton and arrived there in August 1942, with the men being divided between the stations in Hulse Road and Marsh Lane, commanded by Chief Officer Thornton and Chief Officer Scott respectively.

In this city, the Canadians helped with the provision of static water tanks, but crucially assisted the NFS during the trials of the PLUTO pipeline.

Tom Porter, who was serving as a member of the NFS, recalls:

I first met the Canadians when our unit was moved to Testwood. We had always drawn most of our fuel from Testwood before we were transferred there, although we also had access to a pump on a local garage forecourt, and when the Canadians arrived we went with them to draw fuel from the garage.

The late May Belbin, an NFS firewoman from Totton, remembered:

The Canadians came to Southampton, I don't know how many, but there were quite a few. They used to tell us about their families because I suppose they were homesick, which is quite understandable, but also it helped us to get to know them better and they became part of our big family.

Jennifer Turner (née Powell) of Waterside recalls:

When I was young, about eighteen, it was all right that I took up the offer of going to local dances with one of the Canadians. I am sorry but I do not know his name. All the men I met were good to me as a young person and they gave me small gifts, usually consisting of some of their rations, which included sweets. My mother said that they used to talk a lot about their families and that they always acted like real gentlemen. I believe some of the men used to get invited to people's homes for meals, but I can't be sure. I know that one of the firemen was killed in the city, but I only found that out after the war when the story was told to me by an aunt.

Off duty, the Canadians excelled at team competitions at the Testwood site. Jack Coulter again:

We had a tow vehicle and trailer pump and we had to drive forward to a tank. The idea was to disconnect the pump from the truck then get the suction in the water of the tank, lay the hose out and knock down a target with the jet of water. This was a fairly standard type of competition. We Canadians, probably being a little younger and a little more active than the British, were able to compete well and we became the winners of the competition. As a result, we were presented with a trophy. All this was filmed by a crew from Canada working for the National Film Board.

May Belbin wrote: 'We used to have field [sports] days and for that I used to wear my best uniform. We went and served teas from the mobile kitchen that had been donated by the Canadian Red Cross.'

Tom Porter also remembers field days attended by the Canadians:

The thing that struck me was the strength of these men. They were very strong and could pick up a light pump off its trailer and carry it without any trouble. There were handles on the end for the British firemen to lift the pump. Also, another thing that struck me was the way they handled fire gear. When they ran out a hose they never carried the branch (hose) under their arm like we did. They just threw it from one man to the next a bit like throwing a baseball.

The Canadians were often to be seen travelling from Totton to Lepe beach and to Hatchett's Pond, where they carried out various training exercises. As Jack Walters wrote in his book (published in 1977), 'The local division of the Auxiliary Fire Service for example, used Hatchett's Pond for training purposes; so too did the RAF who carried out simulated rescue exercises for Aircrew.'

Distinguished by their larger build and noted for the thigh-high protective service boots they wore, the Canadians proved to be a very popular addition to the multinational wartime community of the New Forest. Their popularity was further enhanced when in early 1943 Leading Fireman Bryce, serving alongside his brother who had also volunteered for service in England, responded to cries for help. A child was in difficulties in the River Test and was in danger of drowning. Without a thought for his own safety, Bryce was quick to jump into action and managed to save the child's life. For this brave act, he was awarded the Humane Medal. Colin Rolfe, the child concerned, was last known to be living

Members of the Fire Service overseas contingent based at Totton. (Author's collection)

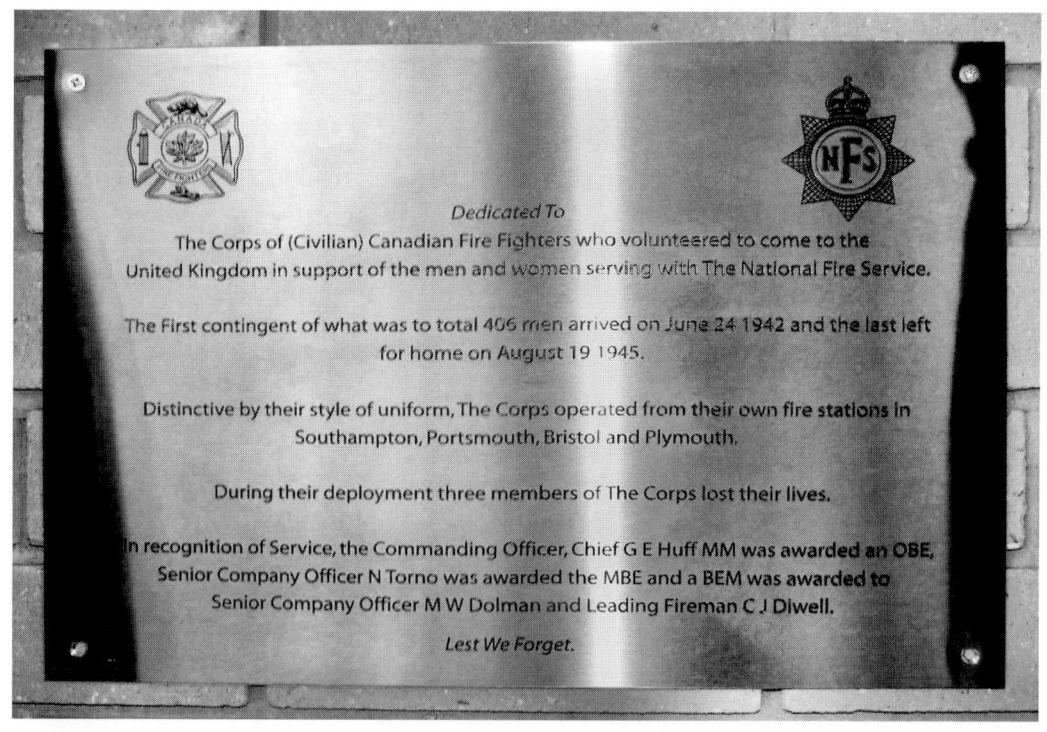

> **Dedicated To**
>
> The Corps of (Civilian) Canadian Fire Fighters who volunteered to come to the United Kingdom in support of the men and women serving with The National Fire Service.
>
> The First contingent of what was to total 406 men arrived on June 24 1942 and the last left for home on August 19 1945.
>
> Distinctive by their style of uniform, The Corps operated from their own fire stations in Southampton, Portsmouth, Bristol and Plymouth.
>
> During their deployment three members of The Corps lost their lives.
>
> In recognition of Service, the Commanding Officer, Chief G E Huff MM was awarded an OBE, Senior Company Officer N Torno was awarded the MBE and a BEM was awarded to Senior Company Officer M W Dolman and Leading Fireman C J Diwell.
>
> *Lest We Forget.*

A memorial plaque dedicated to the men of the Corps of Canadian Firefighters takes pride of place at the headquarters of the Hampshire Fire and Rescue Service. (Author's collection)

Representatives of the Canadian Fire Service unveil the plaque. (Author's collection)

Representatives from Canada with Hampshire Fire Service representatives attended the unveiling of the memorial plaque. (Author's collection)

in London in 2008. During their service on Britain's Home Front, the Canadians suffered five casualties and three deaths. Fireman 'Scotty' Coull, no. T112 of Winnipeg, died in July 1944, a casualty of a flying bomb attack. He is laid to rest in Scotland and at his burial he was given full military honours. Section Leader Lawrence 'Curly' Woodhead, no. T305 from Saskatoon, died in June 1944 when he fell from a speeding fire engine during a training exercise in Southampton.

May Belbin again:

They used to go out on manoeuvres and sometimes the fire engines were overloaded with men. One of the firemen fell off the lorry and was killed. They put his coffin in the hall at Testwood and it was draped with the Canadian flag. We all went down to pay our respects.

Section Leader Alfred LaPierre, no. T212 of Montreal, was also killed in action, and with Lawrence Woodhead was laid to rest in the grounds of the Canadian section of Brookwood Cemetery in Woking.

The Canadian volunteers served until the end of the war. They saw service during the Blitz and were involved in various activities in the New Forest in support of the preparations for the D-Day landings. A fine commemorative plaque in their memory was unveiled in 2008 at Hampshire Fire and Rescue Service Headquarters, Eastleigh.

6
Each Man Gave of His Best

Fire cover was provided at all military camps, fire stations, supply depots, airfields and at other prime locations as the build-up to D-Day began apace. From late 1943, the country's Fire Force Areas (operational areas) were graded into three categories for the purpose of a new operational plan, known as the Colour Scheme. As part of this, reinforcing personnel, many of whom were women, moved into the south of England, including the New Forest.

Blue Areas were considered to be at highest risk, and they were reinforced. These forward areas soon became vast tented cities for Allied troops, with many more Armed Services personnel already stationed on and around the new airfields and of the USAAF and the RAF. Green Areas were classified as being at moderate risk. In the Brown Areas, personnel and equipment were reduced as a result of the prolonged absence of enemy attack. This scheme is relatively unknown, and it is therefore worth exploring it in some detail.

An Operational Memorandum was prepared with great care, and detailed guidance was given to Fire Force Commanders in the Blue, Green and Brown Areas to show them how the scheme was to operate. Fire Force 14, for example, was classified as a Blue Area, so the Fire Force Commander was faced with the immediate prospect of an influx of reinforcing personnel of all ranks, both men and women, and a proportionate increase in the number of appliances. Arthur Stevens recalled:

As the war progressed, preparations began for D-Day and there was a lot of activity in our local area. We were being sent fire service reinforcements from London and the Midlands to strengthen our numbers, and we then were given an extra vehicle which was housed in a garage next door to the station.

One important job which we did was working with some of the Canadians at Lepe near Beaulieu in the New Forest, on the PLUTO pipeline which was being tested under the Solent, and we had to pump fresh water through and it would come out at the other end, that is, on the Isle of Wight.

Throughout the early years of the war the nation's fire services had, it was acknowledged, performed work over and above the call of duty in controlling the thousands of fires caused by enemy air raids. As the plans for the invasion of occupied Europe accelerated in the autumn of 1943, it became clear that the NFS was to take a key role, particularly in those regions of the country from which any attack on the continent was to be launched. In this advanced stage of the war, the needs of the civilian population, whilst still receiving attention, were to be subordinated in the invasion launch areas in favour of the need to assist the armed forces.

A Fire Service convoy stops for a break at a local British Restaurant. (HFRS)

By the time the invasion day dawned, the NFS was ready for all emergencies. During the weeks that followed, all calls for assistance were responded to promptly and each man gave of his best.

A similar set of circumstances had occurred during the late summer of 1943 when Exercise Harlequin had been staged. This exercise involved the marshalling and embarkation of troops and equipment from ports on the south coast, and their journey by sea to within a few miles of the French coast. This 'trailing of their coat', as it was called by the Allied Forces, had evoked no response from the enemy other than a minor raid on Portsmouth on the first night of the exercise, when sixty-three fires were attended by the NFS. The build-up of the armed services and the reinforcement of target areas by the NFS had been carried out in a realistic manner, and many lessons had been learned. These were to prove of tremendous value in the months to come.

Cyril Kendall recorded:

In 1944, one interesting thing was that on all the main roads down the country there were slabs of concrete on the side of the road. We got an order saying that the company, mine was St George's Company, was to go to a particular point for which we were given a map reference. When we arrived, a despatch rider told us to place our trailer pumps on each of the concrete slabs which were placed every so many hundreds of yards apart, and we were to wait there for two hours. Well, we had only been there for a short time when literally hundreds of army lorries convoyed past us on the way to the south of England. Our job was to protect the men and vehicles from fires that might break out in the vehicles, and in fact we did have fun with a couple of ammunition lorries which exploded. No one was hurt and the convoy was really uninterrupted by the fires.

Jill Potter recalls what she saw as an eight-year-old girl:

I saw many fire engines and men in the Forest area for quite some time, and that must have been about the time when all the troops were coming here for what we later knew of course to be in readiness for D-Day. I was told after the war, by the way, that the fire crews were needed to look after the hundreds of military camps which were being filled up with men and equipment and lorries, and all that sort of thing. If my memory serves me well, I did hear of a lorry full of ammunition blowing up near Southampton, so I suppose that's the sort of thing that the fire brigade had to deal with.

Improvements to reinforcement bases were made following Exercise Harlequin, particularly with the knowledge of military movements and the possible contingencies following damage by enemy action to main transport routes. NFS convoys were not to exceed five appliances, because it was considered that larger formations were less likely to be able to overtake military convoys in an emergency. NFS despatch riders were trained on convoy runs and requested to use non-military routes where necessary.

National Fire Service riders and messengers in training. (NFRS)

Certain roads in the Forest were made one-way only by the military authorities to meet the needs of service traffic in embarkation and back areas. This necessitated changes in predetermined attendance arrangements, as stations were frequently rendered much more remote from certain risks as a result of the roundabout routes that had to be taken. Predetermined attendances also had to be arranged for camps and vehicle parks. In view of the closure of certain roads it was vital that despatch riders should gain knowledge of alternative routes for convoy purposes. The despatch riders who had been transferred under the Colour Scheme also had to become fully acquainted with local topography. Frequent reinforcing exercises were accordingly arranged between neighbouring areas and regions so that personnel could undertake exercises focusing on the routes they should follow and the location of rendezvous points and reinforcement bases.

The fact that members of the NFS lived for months under canvas with the army in the camps was probably the best demonstration of the liaison that existed between the two services. During Exercise Harlequin, units of the Army Fire Service (AFS) were moved down to the southern part of the area for the purpose of supplementing existing NFS cover. These units worked in very close cooperation with the NFS and were actually mobilised through the nearest Sub-Divisional Control. Arrangements were made so that AFS units could be called upon to assist at fires that did not involve military establishments. This practice helped to train the army in practical fire-fighting, and many exercises were carried out in the Forest with sections of the AFS. Training included water relaying over open country or in built-up areas for the purpose of gaining experience in ramping, positioning of pumps and various traffic problems. What were known as pipeline exercises were organised at Hatchett's Pond, and there were also exercises involving the use of fireboats on Southampton Water. Ronald Tilling, a former dock worker, wrote:

> *Positioned right round the docks at Southampton were many fire pumps and probably a couple of hundred men ready to assist if anything happened when we were loading stores, fuel and vehicles onto the assortment of craft that had tied up here in the weeks prior to 6 June.*

> *I know that fireboats based in Southampton Water went out many times to deal with fire problems on some of the ships in the Solent armada.*

Air support for the invasion presented its own additional risk to the NFS. Hampshire, and in particular the New Forest, was among the most densely populated military conurbations during the build-up to D-Day, and already had a number of permanent and temporary airfields. The airfields were used by many types of British and American aircraft, and these were mainly fighters, including the Typhoon and Hurricane, and fighter-bombers such as the P47 Thunderbolt. However, larger aircraft including the Wellington, Flying Fortress and Halifax, were also flying out of the area.

The numbers of aircraft increased as the clock counted down to 6 June, and so too did the number of sorties from every airfield. This increased aircraft presence brought with it some major challenges for the NFS, and inevitably many calls during the months of April, May and June 1944 were to plane crashes. In fact, during this period there were fifty-two recorded crashes within the tight-knit network of airfields in south and west Hampshire alone. In contrast, only forty-seven call outs to crashes were recorded in the previous year to December 1943. It must be remembered that many of the airfields were in very close proximity to one another and airspace was at a premium: on more than one occasion collisions took place.

RAF Ibsley was one of the larger permanent airfields, and there are still signs of wartime occupation despite much of the site now being a peaceful nature reserve. It was not always so quiet: one summer morning in 1944 a fighter aircraft crashed shortly after take-off from the main north–south concrete runway. Immediately, a call was sent to the local NFS station and simultaneously a call was put out to the USAAF crash tender stationed on the airfield. As the American vehicle arrived on the scene, the bomb payload on the stricken aircraft exploded, setting both the aircraft and the crash tender alight. Fortunately, the pilot escaped the mayhem, but the tender crew lost their lives.

On 29 June in the same year, a P47 Thunderbolt crashed and demolished a bungalow not far from the Christchurch airfield at Somerford, then several

The aircraft crash close to the airfield at Christchurch. (HFRS)

hours later the same pilot in another aircraft took off from the same aerodrome and crashed again, this time blowing up the fire appliance which had been on stand-by after the previous incident. The blast from the explosion brought down a second aircraft that had taken off at the same time. The fires and resulting damage caused by exploding bombs killed fourteen people including two civilians, one of whom was a fireman. Among the twenty-two who were injured, two were firemen.

In addition to dealing with aviation-related incidents, the firemen providing cover for the military during the build-up to D-Day also dealt with call outs to heath and gorse fires which threatened ammunition dumps, stores and the 'tented cities' which housed thousands of troops. As one fireman commented, 'Travelling through the county we saw what seemed like hundreds of trailer pumps, thousands of tented camps for the Army and American Thunderbolts flying overhead. What a sight and one I will never forget.'

In Germany, meanwhile, the Führer had on 16 May ordered the long-range V-1 (Vengeance Weapon, Fzg 76) bombardment of England to commence in June. His order stated that 'The bombardment would open like a thunderclap by night.'

Notes from the Fire Force diary capture the mood of the times:

7 June 1944
There had been no enemy action during the previous night although large concentrations of Allied aircraft had continued operations from this country. One interesting feature of the previous evening had been the flight over HQ of hundreds of four-engine bombers, each one towing a large glider at an altitude of about 1000 feet.
These gliders are capable of carrying a load of 30 fully armed soldiers. Large convoys of re-enforcements, lorries, tanks, bulldozers and steamrollers were encountered on the roads.

8 June 1944
500 German prisoners were landed and selected prisoners were interrogated by Intelligence Officers. An NFS officer who witnessed the landing commented on the arrogant bearing of these prisoners.

After the frenetic activity of the early months of 1944, which culminated in the mass movement of military men and machines out of the Blue Zone from 6 June, the Fire Services then faced the unknown terrors of the flying bombs. But by September the tide was turning, and a more upbeat mood swept the country.

8 September 1944
As decreed by Adolph [sic] Hitler, the first V-1 rockets were launched against London. This rocket was only accurate to within a ten-mile radius of the target and was vulnerable to anti-aircraft fire. More than half the rockets fired at England were brought down by the Anti-Aircraft gun batteries along the south coast. Nevertheless, the damage caused

by those rockets which penetrated the AA screen and arrived at the targets, was substantial and casualties exceeded 6000 dead.
[NB. The later variant, the V-2 rocket arrived silently, unlike its noisy predecessor, and over 500 of these reached London, killing a total of 2,724 people.]

Another note, dated 11 September 1944, was entered into the Fire Force Log Book:

The Allied invasion of the Continent has brought many pleasant surprises, not the least of which is the lack of enemy retaliation on the country. Everyone had expected at the outset that there would have been heavy bombing attacks along the south coast and with the arrival of the flying bomb, some serious situations could have developed very easily. As things have gone however, the prospect of enemy air activity is receding fast and the time has come for the personnel who were sent to reinforce this Area in the early part of the year, to return to the North of England.

Many requests were received by the Regional Commissioner's Office from both firemen and firewomen who asked to be allowed to stay in the south. However, only in exceptional cases was permission granted, and those who were accepted had to forfeit all right to lodging allowances, reverting to the same status as those whose homes were in the area. When repatriation began, the vast majority of firemen and women were sent in phases from their various fire stations to the Alresford Reinforcement Base near Winchester in Hampshire, from where they were taken the 10 miles by road to Alton railway station for onward travel to other parts of the country.

The level of cover given by the Colour Scheme was maintained until November 1944, when the progress of the war dictated that it be phased out and personnel returned to their respective forces. Many friendships were forged between fellow firefighters who had come together in a unique set of circumstances to play their part in safeguarding potentially vulnerable parts

In memoriam. This statue can be seen at Hampshire Fire and Rescue headquarters in Eastleigh. (HFRS)

of the country, as well as providing a fire protection 'insurance policy' for the hundreds of thousands of men who were encamped throughout the south on the eve of the liberation of occupied Europe. Words alone cannot begin to describe the sometimes arduous, but always purposeful, journey that was undertaken by the nation's Fire Services between 1937 and the final months of the war.

7

A Long Battle in the Skies

Towards the end of the First World War, General Jan Smuts, the distinguished South African-born soldier, was the chair of a committee which was tasked with looking at measures for Britain's Home Defence, for it was clear that much had been learnt during the previous years of conflict about the nation's capabilities and inabilities.

It was Smuts who was quoted as saying that 'The day might not be far off when aerial operations may become the principal operations of war, to which the older forms of military operations may become secondary and subordinate.' He went on to make the recommendation that the existing Royal Flying Corps (RFC) should be amalgamated with the Royal Naval Air Squadron, and this became a reality in April 1918. The RAF was formed just seven months before the 11 November 1918 Armistice, at which time it was the largest air service in the world with more than 22,000 aircraft at its disposal, many of which were built in Hampshire.

East Boldre Airfield in the New Forest, which opened in 1910 for pleasure flying, was closed just a year or so later and then reopened in 1915 as Flying Training School, RFC Beaulieu. Expansion of the site in 1917 included an additional three hangars as well as workshops and barracks.

RFC Beaulieu hosted 16 Training Squadron, flying Avro 504s, B.E.2cs and Curtiss Jennys, and this squadron arrived in December 1916. In November 1917, 59 Squadron, which flew Sopwith Camels, arrived; 79 Squadron with Sopwith Dolphins arrived in August 1917, leaving in February 1918; 84 Squadron was formed in January 1917 with B.E.2cs and B.E.12as, departing in March of the same year; 103 Squadron with various types of plane formed in

September 1917 and left the same month; 117 Squadron with DH.4s and R.E.8s was formed in January 1918 and disbanded in July 1918; and finally 29 Training Depot Station was formed in July 1918 from 59 Squadron and 79 Squadron.

During the summer of 1919, Hugh Trenchard worked on the challenging task of completing the RAF's demobilisation and establishing it on a peace-time basis. There was a huge post-war budget earmarked for the demolition of existing airfield infrastructures at the end of hostilities, and it was proposed that the RAF would dramatically reduce in size, from 188 squadrons to around twenty-five. Beaulieu was one of many stations that were no longer needed as the RAF reorganised for its new operational conditions, and it was abandoned just a few months after the end of the war, in 1919. Worth noting, however, is that nearby Calshot, on the spit at the end of Southampton Water close to Lepe, in use as a flying boat base from 1913, remained operational. It was officially commissioned in February 1922 as RAF Calshot.

It was also during this time that the new RAF officer ranks were decided upon, despite some opposition from members of the Army Council. Trenchard was regraded from Major General to Air Vice Marshal, then promoted to Air Marshal a few days later.

By the autumn of 1919, the effects of Lloyd George's 'Ten Year Rule' were causing Trenchard some difficulty as he sought to develop the institutions of the RAF. Simply put, the Ten Year Rule was based on a premise that a war-weary world would not engage in any further conflict for a least a decade. Trenchard had to argue against the view that the Army and Royal Navy should provide support services and education, leaving the RAF to focus only on flying training. He viewed this idea as a precursor to the break-up of the RAF, and in spite of the cost he wanted his own institutions, which would develop airmanship and engender the spirit of the air. Although Trenchard attained a measure of financial security, the future of the RAF was far from assured. He judged that the chief threat to his position came from the new First Sea Lord, Admiral Beatty. And so, seeking to take the initiative, Trenchard arranged to meet him. Arguing that the 'air is one and indivisible', Trenchard put forward a case for an air force with its own strategic role, which would also control army and navy cooperation squadrons. Perhaps not surprisingly,

Beatty did not accept this argument, so Hugh Trenchard resorted to asking for a twelve-month amnesty before changes were made. This request appealed to Beatty's sense of fair play and he agreed to it, giving Trenchard until the end of 1920 to produce detailed plans. It was around this time that Trenchard indicated to Beatty that control over some supporting elements of naval aviation might be returned to the Admiralty. Trenchard also offered Beatty the option of locating Air Ministry staff who worked with naval aviation at the Admiralty. Beatty declined the offer and later, when no transfer of any naval aviation assets occurred, came to the view that Trenchard had acted in bad faith.

Having convinced Churchill of his case, Trenchard oversaw the founding of the RAF (Cadet) College at Cranwell as the world's first military air academy. Later, in 1920, he inaugurated the Aircraft Apprentice scheme, which provided the RAF with specialist ground crew. He also sought to secure the future of the RAF by finding an active fighting role for the new service, and also in 1920 he successfully argued that the service should take the lead during operations to restore peace in Somaliland. The success of this small air action allowed Trenchard to put the case for the RAF's policing of the Empire. Controversially, earlier the same year he had written that the RAF could even suppress industrial disturbances or uprisings in mainland Britain. The idea was not to Churchill's liking, and he instructed Trenchard not to refer to this proposal again.

During the early 1920s, the continued independent existence of the RAF and its control of naval aviation were subject to a series of governmental reviews. The Balfour report of 1921, the Geddes Axe of 1922 and the Salisbury Committee of 1923 all found in favour of the RAF, despite lobbying from the Admiralty and opposition in Parliament. On every occasion, Hugh Trenchard and his staff officers worked to prove that the RAF provided good value for money and was required for the long-term strategic security of the United Kingdom.

Some media observers at the time referred to a poem (it is displayed at RAF Cranwell), apparently written in 1797, as the inspiration behind those who were for the maintenance and enhancement of an effective air defence.

The time will come when thou shalt lift thine eyes
To watch a long drawn battle in the skies
While aged peasants too amazed for words
Stare at the flying fleets of wondrous birds
England so long the mistress of the sea
Where winds and waves confess her sovereignty
Her ancient triumph yet on high shall bear
And reign, the sovereign of the conquered air.

In 1922 the RAF was given control of all British Forces in Iraq. It also carried out Imperial air policing over India's North-West Frontier province. In the same year, the RAF Staff College at Andover, Hampshire, was set up to provide RAF-specific training for middle-ranking officers. Yet the RAF still only had twelve squadrons on airfields across the country, very unlike the situation in France – which possessed the best-equipped air force in Europe.

The story of the fledgling years of the RAF is not too dissimilar to its story in the twenty-first century, for it includes unworkable ideas, political careers, budget cuts and indecision, underlined by improvements in some areas.

Under Stanley Baldwin's government of 1923–4, agreement was reached on the creation of a Home Defence Air Force and the provision of mobile and fixed sound locators (an early radar system). Later, and still under Baldwin, who returned to power from late 1924, new bomber stations were grouped geographically: the areas included Hampshire. Less than two decades later the New Forest was to accommodate a network of airfields, or air stations as they were also called, in addition to the existing flying boat station at Calshot and a site at Christchurch, all of which played a vital role in the preparations for and launch of D-Day in 1944.

The Ten Year Rule was abolished in 1932. It was acknowledged that the RAF was in a position of weakness with only a few aircraft, some of which were obsolete. New permanent aerodrome building began under a scheme, commonly known as the Expansion Programme, in 1934, in recognition of the long overdue need for 'permanent' bases for the RAF, which was to increase in strength in a phased manner over the coming years. These new aerodromes were built to a standard design with variations to suit local conditions. Each site included most of the same technical buildings, including water tower, control tower, station headquarters, parachute store, workshops, central heating station, bomb and ammunition stores, motor transport pool and operations block, engine house, guardroom, fire engine garage, fuel store and gunnery range. In addition, there were offices, locker rooms, wireless rooms and aircraft equipment stores, hangars, accommodation, canteens, washrooms and rest rooms.

In the airfield summaries that follow, please note that the following abbreviations are used: NVR (no visible remains); SVR (some visible remains).

Christchurch
Pundit code XC (the identity code of the airfield: a beacon was set to flash the relevant letter or letters to confirm the name of the aerodrome to aircraft overhead). Already established at the outbreak of the Second World War, the aerodrome had an interesting history spanning the previous two decades. On the boundary of the New Forest, Christchurch was in Hampshire at the time; now it is in Dorset as a consequence of boundary changes. The runways included grass, concrete and steel matting, a total of five in all. There were five hangars, including three 'blister' types in preparation for war service. It acted as a satellite for nearby Hurn and Ibsley airfields under No. 10 Group, Fighter Command. It became operational in 1940.
(NVR)

Ibsley
Pundit code IB, call sign LARDIT. This airfield was built by various contractors and opened in early 1941, with three tarmac runway sites and twelve hangars. Many variants of the Spitfire and also the Hurricane Mk I flew from Ibsley. Based here were 32, 66, 118, 129, 165, 234, 263, 302, 310, 312, 313, 421, 453, 501, 504 and 616 Squadrons. It transferred between the RAF and the USAAF on two occasions.
(SVR, in private ownership)

A German aerial photograph of Christchurch Airfield. (Author's collection)

The former control or watch tower at Ibsley. (Author's collection)

Ibsley: The Northern Cupola on the site of the former airfield. (NFNPA)

Beaulieu

Pundit code BU, call sign ARCHEBACK. Beaulieu Heath was on the opposite side of the road to the First World War East Boldre airfield, and was opened in the autumn of 1942 having been built by various contractors to the standard three runway design. To begin with it had two T2 hangars and a single blister type, and it was variously home to 257, 263 and 486 Squadrons flying Typhoons and Tempests. In the early days most personnel had tented accommodation, and the operations room and control tower were of temporary construction. No. 224 Squadron, flying Liberator 111As, arrived in September to bolster the U-boat offensive in the Bay of Biscay. Halifaxes of 405 and 158 Squadrons, Royal Canadian Air Force, arrived to take part in strikes against enemy shipping. Later in the war, in the post D-Day period, various aircraft including B26 Marauders flew into this airfield on the way to France. Lysanders carrying SOE agents also flew from Beaulieu, the nearby village being home to various training establishments.

Beaulieu Airfield was put under the control of the USAAF in May 1944 and reverted to RAF control in September of the same year.
(SVR)

Holmsley South

Pundit code HM; call sign RECESS. This airfield was built by John Laing and Son Ltd and opened under Coastal Command in September 1942. With three runways and five T2 hangars it was a large aerodrome, flying Spitfires, Typhoons and Mustangs. It passed to the USAAF in June 1944 and then to RAF Transport Command in October 1944.
(SVR)

Hurn

Pundit code KU. This was a large aerodrome, with three concrete runways and seventeen hangars including for T2 types. It hosted Typhoons and Mosquitoes from 125, 164, 181, 182, 183, 193, 197, 198, 247, 257, 263 and 266 Squadrons. Opened in summer 1941, the site is now Bournemouth International Airport.
(SVR)

An aerial view of part of Beaulieu Estate. (Beaulieu Estate)

418 Squadron Royal Canadian Air Force at Holmsley. (John Leavesley)

An aerial photograph of a section of the former Stoney Cross airfield. (© Forest Research, based on Cambridge University Technical Services)

Needs Oar Point

Pundit code NI. This was opened in April 1944, for D-Day only, right on the coast at St Leonard's in the New Forest. The site had two runways of steel matting and four Blister hangars. It flew Typhoons from 193 and 197 Squadrons. Domestic accommodation was in tents, and the nearby farmhouse at Park Farm was used for units including Intelligence and Radio.
(SVR, in private ownership)

Stoney Cross

Pundit code SS. Call sign IRONWORK. Situated in the north of the Forest, Stoney Cross was opened in November 1942, although at that time it was still under construction by George Wimpey and Co. Ltd. With a typical three concrete runway layout, this site was originally conceived to serve as a 'secret' airfield, deliberately devoid of any of the usual facilities and with camouflaged hides for aircraft, although the exact reason it was to be secret remains open to conjecture. It was subsequently designated as an advance base for both fighters and bombers, and in the process it expanded from about 500 to 900 acres, yet its construction was delayed because of disagreements over how much compensation was to be paid to commoners who grazed their cattle on the site. An agreement was eventually reached, and the six-month delay in starting work was overlooked by the authorities. The agreement to pay compensation at the rate of 2s 6d per acre was subsequently cancelled under a War Requisitions Act.

Four new generation T2 hangars were erected, as were six blister types. Flying Hurricanes, Venturas, Stirlings and the widely criticised Albermarles from 175, 297 and 299 Squadrons were based here. Stoney Cross was operated by the RAF and the USAAF.

There are several features at the south-eastern end of the airfield immediately adjacent to the main A31 that may represent features of an anti-aircraft site. These include a possible searchlight emplacement, a gun-laying radar position, a radio mast and foxholes. These features are not recorded on the RAF maps of the airfield, but further investigation may be able to more positively identify them.

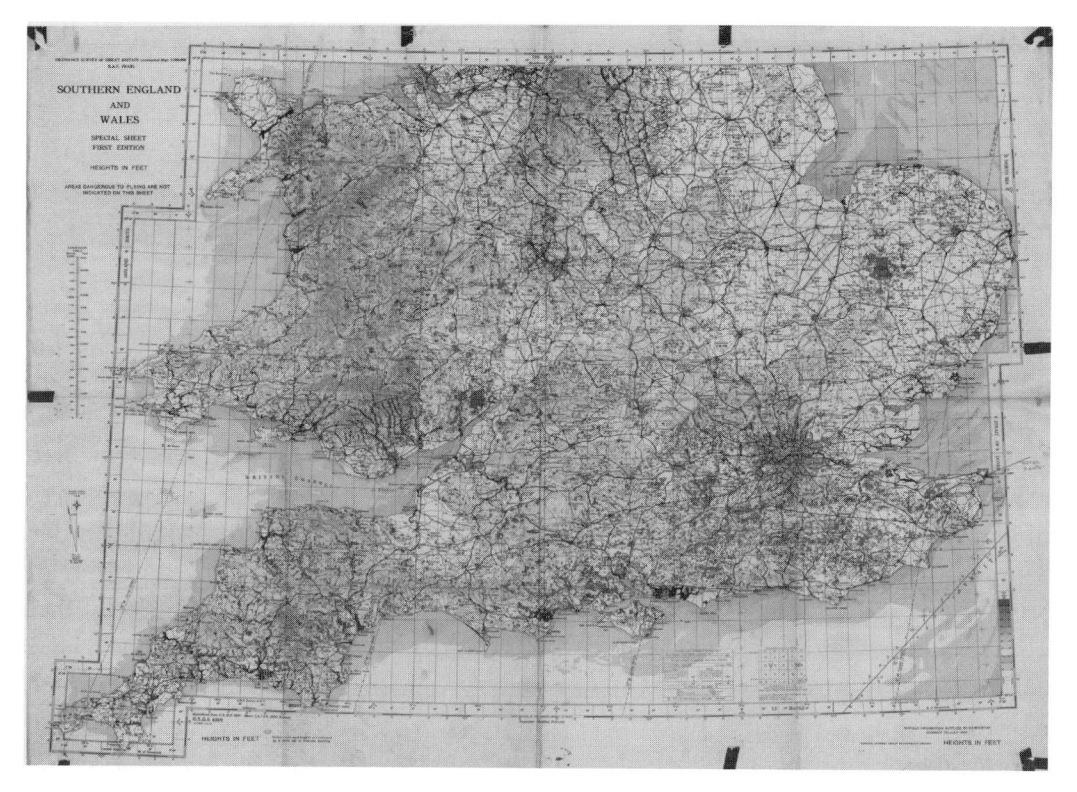

An early war map showing several of the Forest airfields. (Author's collection)

An ancillary site of Stoney Cross airfield, the sick quarters at Castle Malwood, was built to accommodate ill and injured staff. Such facilities were a necessary feature of any military structure, and consisted of wards, a mortuary, an ambulance garage and nursing staff quarters. The RAF site plan refers to an HF (high frequency) transmitting station located immediately east of this area.

Stoney Cross airfield was released by the War Ministry in 1948 and largely demolished a few years later. As with many sites around the New Forest, it is possible that this demolition was only surface deep, leaving many platforms and foundations intact. The site of the sick quarters presently lies alongside the A31, which will almost certainly have disrupted the site when it was made into a dual carriageway in the 1960s. The HF station may conceivably have been a

particularly tall structure, therefore leaving deep foundations.
(SVR)

Winkton
Pundit code XT, call sign DRAINSINK. This was an advanced landing ground for D-Day only, with two steel matting runways and four blister-type hangars. It was used by the USAAF under the control of 11 Group, RAF Fighter Command;. Opened in March 1944, it was closed less than a year later.
(SVR, in private ownership)

Calshot
Call sign STAMMER. Situated on the spit at the end of Southampton Water, Calshot entered the war for flying boat training, using the Singapore and Stranraer biplane flying boats of 201, 209 and 240 Squadrons. It was a service centre for Sunderlands and an operational base for Air Sea Rescue launches. The original flying boat sheds and some original buildings remain in use. One of the most intriguing aspects of Calshot's wartime history is its use as a base for Heinkel HE 115 Floatplanes. A number of these enemy planes were flown to England by Norwegian pilots and at least one was subsequently pressed into service by British Intelligence. We know that one of the Heinkels completed thirty-eight missions into enemy territory. We also know that the two floats on the plane were fitted with electric motors so that when the main engines were cut, the plane could manoeuvre quietly through the water. The floats were hollowed out and fitted with seats and a small protective glass shield. An agent would sit in each one, making it easier to transfer to a boat or the shore.
(SVR)

Sway
This almost forgotten but vital emergency landing ground (ELG) was used sporadically for just a few months in 1944 and, according to locals, offered no facilities except a grass strip and a guard hut. Aircraft were moved here from time to time from Christchurch, until the enemy bombed Sway in a light attack.
(NVR, in private ownership)

Bisterne
This site was surveyed in 1943 and was deemed suitable for service as an ALG, for use solely as part of the D-Day campaign. Opened in September 1943, basic facilities comprised two steel mesh air strips, hard standings and an aircraft marshalling area. Four blister hangars were erected, providing better cover for aircraft than the tents provided for the crews. Flying the P-47s of 371st Fighter Group, USAAF, from April 1944, it was not long before the mesh tracking became rutted and the site had to be temporarily closed for reconstruction. The Thunderbolts moved to Ibsley, before returning on 1 May 1944. The 371st continued its assaults on occupied Europe. Post D-Day the site was soon abandoned, and it was derelict by July 1944.
(NVR, in private ownership)

Pylewell, also known as Lymington
This ALG was created on the Pylewell Estate, which was already being used by other armed services units. Great swathes of woodland were removed to lay steel mesh for two temporary runways on Snooks Farm and a number of blister hangars were erected. The 9th Tactical Air Command of the USAAF arrived in March 1944 with P47 Thunderbolts, and domestic accommodation was mainly under canvas. The site was effectively stood down in July 1944 and returned to farmland.

For the most part, all new permanent aerodromes built after the outbreak of war used the dispersal principle of siting various key buildings at a distance from the main runway and hangar complex, as a safety measure in case of concentrated bombing by an enemy. For example, the barns at the junction of Shotts Lane and Lisle Court Road, East End, near Lymington, were used as debriefing rooms.
(NVR in private ownership)

RAF Sopley
A ground control intercept (GCI) radar station was established at Sopley near Bransgore (on land requisitioned from the Manners Estate) in December 1940. The first installation was a mobile unit designed to be set up in just twelve hours

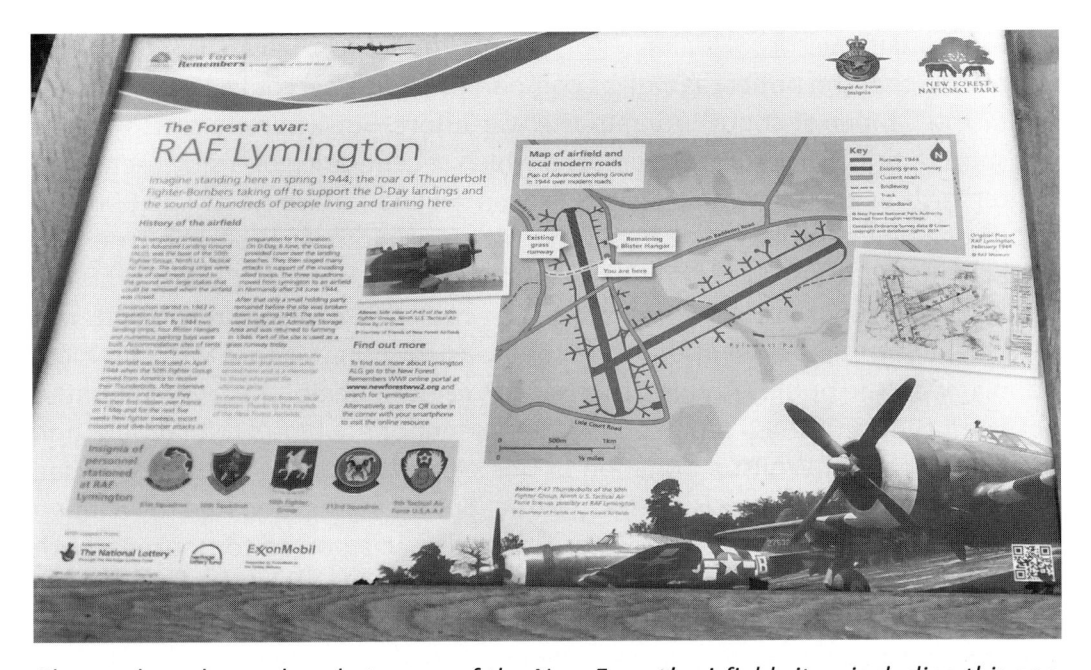

Plaques have been placed at many of the New Forest's airfield sites, including this one at Lymington. Each plaque includes detailed information about the site. (Author's collection)

and capable of operating all day every day. It was designed to identify enemy bombers and guide home searchlights and night fighter interceptors towards them. RAF Sopley served the night fighter squadrons based at RAF Middle Wallop (near Andover, Hampshire) and nearby RAF Hurn throughout the war. The antenna arrangement used here was so successful that its style was used at several other GCI (RADAR) stations, and Sopley achieved one of the highest success rates of intercepts of any GCI station in the war. In 1941 the installation was upgraded to an 'intermediate transportable' type, and in 1943 Sopley was made into a permanent station with a fixed antenna. Construction took place in an adjacent field, and consisted of large brick buildings for operations rooms and equipment with a permanent Type 7 radar antenna alongside.

(NVR. The site is a business park and the home of Friends of the New Forest Airfields. Contact them for more information)

In 1940, Lord Beaverbrook, Minister of Aircraft Production, began promoting the suggestion that the public, as well as companies and clubs, could pay for aircraft under the banner of contributing to the war effort. But where to start was the question. A price structure was created which set the price of a single-engined fighter such as the Spitfire at £5,000, a twin-engined machine at £20,000 and a four-engined aeroplane at £40,000. These sums did not reflect the true cost of each, but were set at a level that was considered would be attractive to and achievable by fundraisers. For example, the actual cost of a Spitfire in 1940, was £9,850, give or take a few pounds, and it was this aircraft that was the most popular with the public. About a thousand Presentation Spitfires were donated between 1940 and 1942, representing 11 per cent of the type's total production during the period. Whilst a donation of one or perhaps two aircraft was usual, a whole squadron comprising forty-three Spitfires was donated by Queen Wilhelmina of the Netherlands. Betty Wait, who was posted to Bournemouth during the war, remembers the details of this donation, which was not widely known until the end of the war. Word got around in the WAAF's canteen, and a loud cheer went up one evening at dinner. 'We thought that this was a good omen for Great Britain and a real boost to our boys in blue,' she said.

The Buy a Spitfire Fund was a nationwide appeal, with Hampshire's effort being launched by the Mayor of Winchester. There was also a call made to farmers for the 'Hampshire Agricultural Fighter Plane'. Brockenhurst, in the New Forest, excelled by raising many thousands of pounds during various Fund weeks, and the community helped towards the cost of 'The New Forest Spitfire', which became a reality within a year of the appeal's launch. Various newspapers competed to raise more money than their rivals, and the local media, including the *Daily Echo* from Southampton, did their bit to champion the cause. Tom Amis sold vegetables at the roadside outside his parents' home in Dibden. 'I collected about four shillings, which I was really pleased about. The thought that something I did helped to buy a Spitfire made me proud in a funny sort of way, and when I saw dogfights I often wondered if any of the planes was one I helped to buy.'

Apart from helping the war effort, the fundraisers got to see their assigned name painted on the fuselage of the aircraft, close to the cockpit. The aircraft,

WAR WEAPONS WEEK. BROCKENHURST.
May 17th—24th, 1941.

OFFICIAL PROGRAMME OF EVENTS.

17th, Saturday.   11 a.m.   Opening Ceremony at Morant Hall.
Speakers—Colonel J. D. Mills, M.P., Colonel V. W. Roche. Followed by a **Military Display** in the Car Park and a **PROCESSION** through the village.

2.30 p.m.   Cricket Match—Brockenhurst v. Army.

7.30 p.m.   Grand Dance, Morant Hall—Moderniques Band.
Prizes 4 War Saving Certificates. Entrance 2/6.

18th, Sunday.   11 a.m.   United Service at the Parish Church.

19th, Monday.   8 p.m.   Special Boxing Exhibition at Morant Hall.
Tickets 3/-, 2/-, 1/-.   (by permission of A.B.A.)

20th, Tuesday.   6 to 9 p.m.   Table Tennis (Knock-out) Competition at the New Forest Club. Entries 6d. to be made before 6 p.m. at the Estate Offices or at the Club.

21st, Wednesday.   2.30 p.m.   Whist Drive at New Forest Club. Entrance 1/-

8.0 p.m.   **GRAND CONCERT & CABARET.** at Morant Hall. Stage Band, Community Singing, Songs, Tap Dancing, Pipers, Comic Sketch, etc. Entrance 3/-, 2/- 1/-.
The War Weapons Week Draw will be made during the evening.

22nd, Thursday.   All day Golf Competition (Open) at Brokenhurst Manor Golf Club—PUTTING IN GAS MASKS.
Entrance 6d. Prizes—War Savings Stamps, etc.

7.30 p.m.   Whist Drive at Morant Hall. Entrance-1/3d. Prizes

23rd, Friday.   6.15 & 8.15 p.m.   Cinema at Morant Hall—"Oh Mr. Porter" (Will Hay), Mickey Mouse, etc.
6.15 p.m.—Entrance 1/-, children 6d.
8.15 p.m.—Entrance 2/-, 1/-, 6d.

24th, Saturday.   2-5 p.m.   Children's Sports at County High School.
An array of Sideshows. Entrance—Adults 3d., Pupils 1d.

8 p.m.   Special Dance at Morant Hall—Moderniques Band. Entrance 2/6. Prizes—4 War Savings Certificates.

During the whole week there will be an Open Golf Competition at Brokenhurst Manor Golf Club. Entrance 1/- a Card.

All profits on Entertainments during the Week will be invested in Government Securities for the Brockenhurst Nursing Association.

Brockenhurst War Weapons Week. (Author's collection)

the men who flew them, those that maintained them, the women of the Women's Auxiliary Air Force (WAAFs) and all those involved in operational duties on the Forest airfields, just like their counterparts throughout the country, are remembered for going 'Through adversity to the stars', *'Per ardua ad astra'*.

8
IN THIS GREAT STRUGGLE

In 1939, at the request of Walter Elliot, Minister of Health, local authorities were preparing to make a survey of available housing accommodation as part of the plan for 'transferring' children and others in an emergency to the homes of those who were willing to take care of them. At the time the New Forest was considered a safe haven for evacuees from local towns, such as Southampton, as well as those from farther afield in the Midlands and the north of England. This was despite the highly visible war construction programme that was under way throughout the area.

The evacuees were at the forefront of an 'invasion of strangers', as one local resident called it in a letter to a local newspaper, and although many youngsters returned home during the period of the 'phoney war', the population of the Forest continued to increase month on month. Some evacuee children returned to the area when the Blitz began, but their numbers were small compared to the large-scale influx of personnel from the armed services, Civil Defence and the Home Guard. Of the Women's Land Army (WLA), a commentator wrote:

> *There I saw girls from the cities, mostly from London, girls who had been shorthand typists, clerks and shop assistants, learning how to milk and do dairy farming, how to work in the fields and so on. They were a healthy and happy bunch of girls. And those girls were in the advance guard of what can reasonably be called a Land Army.*

Noreen Cooper was in the WLA, and her list of 'jobs to be done' makes exhausting reading:

Everything stops for tea for members of the local Timber Corps. (NARA)

Hard at work on the land: members of the Women's Land Army – recreated by Nick Halling. (Nick Halling)

IN THIS GREAT STRUGGLE

Lend a hand on the land. (Nick Halling)

Every piece of available land was cultivated in Lymington, as elsewhere. (Wayne Johnson)

Members of the Timber Corps. (NARA)

Apart from milking and mucking out, the girls were expected to plant and pick up potatoes, look after the mangolds [root vegetables mainly used as cattle food] and sugar beet harvests, hay making, rick making, stoking, threshing and bagging wheat, pea picking, carrot harvesting and bagging, sprout picking, kale cutting, dung spreading and drawing straw for thatching. We were also responsible for fruit picking, feeding the cows, loading and unloading full and empty milk churns, thistle cutting, dock pulling, rat catching, harnessing and working with horses, shepherding sheep and white washing the milk sheds. Oh, and keeping out of the way of lecherous farmers.

Well, we had to get the milking done and then we sat on the fence and watched the convoys passing. We were waving, really high spirited and we shouted out 'Good Luck' to the men. It was an exciting but nevertheless strange time really. Many of those poor chaps of course would be killed before the eventual end of the war, but for that moment in time there was so much exuberance and good feeling, almost euphoria after the long slog of the previous years of war, and now we knew the end could well be in sight.

Not all land acquisition took place for military purposes. In 1941, the War Agricultural Committee drew up plans to reseed large areas of grazing land to improve the quality of the grass. Although not particularly successful, this was followed by the decision to cultivate large areas of open grazing land in 1944, so that crops and vegetables could be grown.

Away from the farms, at various sites around the New Forest, groups of girls worked alongside men in forest management tasks such as brush burning, sawing and measuring. The American photojournalist turned war correspondent Lee Miller recorded in her 1943 article 'Children of the New Forest' that 'They are the girls of the Timber Corps. Most of them are in their teens or twenties, many of them have taken a degree at University, fifty percent brain, fifty percent brawn, plus plenty of initiative, is the formula for a good forester.' Twenty-nine million cubic feet of timber was earmarked for felling at the outbreak of war, both in the Crown Estates and other forests, with the New Forest being a key source of supply. The Corps helped to clear the undergrowth in these woods, and then trimmed the trees that were felled by the lumberjacks. The girls learnt general forestry skills, sawmill management and tractor driving, and opportunities existed (much more so in the Timber Corps than in the WLA) for roles of greater responsibility, such as supervisor.

Holmsley Mill on the A35 between Lyndhurst and Christchurch was one of the central hubs for the Timber Corps in the New Forest during the Second World War, and it is still a working mill. The nearby railway station (the station house is now a restaurant) was the drop off and collection point not just for WLA and Timber Corps members, but also for service personnel stationed at Holmsley South Airfield.

Fraternisation between men and women was discouraged, but as Mary Weller recalled:

One night at our lodgings in Burley, we heard noises outside. Three of us marched outside straight into a few chaps from the local airfield. They were embarrassed at being caught out, but they just hoped to 'catch sight of some pretty girls' and maybe go to the cinema one evening. It was all very clumsy, but very innocent. These men were too afraid to knock on the door and ask us out, instead they hung around outside, but they were too noisy and didn't bargain on three strong and confident lassies taking charge of the situation. Did we go to the cinema after all that? Sadly, the men were posted a day or two later, never to be seen again. Life at the time was just so many twists and turns, but we were all in the great struggle together and we had to learn to deal with it.

The Forest as it is today has been shaped by the wartime felling of trees and post war replanting, as well as by the heavy footprint of the massive wartime construction programme. Mary Weller was just one of thousands of women who were called into service and posted to the New Forest; part of a national sisterhood of fifteen million who were conscripted into war production, the armed services, other support services and voluntary work. The government was freely given powers under the National Service (No. 2) Act December 1941

The former station at Holmsley welcomed thousands of military personnel during the war years. (Author's collection)

The road at Holmsley runs along the original railway track footprint on its way to Beaulieu. Note the line of the track under the railway bridge at Holmsley. (Author's collection)

to conscript suitable classes of women for the Forces and through the Registration for Employment Order, to direct women to any civilian employment in which they might be needed.

In October 1939, the number of women on the register of unemployed increased by nearly 200,000, at a time when unemployment amongst men was falling. This was in part because many women were engaged in voluntary work and were therefore not registered for work. Dorothy Sayer, originally of Walkford, was a volunteer hospital visitor and later served as an Auxiliary Territorial Service despatch rider. 'There was no grumbling or resentment about being called up, we all wanted to do our bit, but there was certainly a lot of grumbling and discontent from impatience and over-enthusiasm to get started in our wartime roles.' One commentator recorded:

> *A woman who has made up her mind, following an appeal to her emotions, that she will present herself for national service, leave home, go wherever she is sent and do whatever is required of her, all at some self-sacrifice, feels irritated and frustrated when she is told by some harassed official that she is not wanted at this time.*

Elsa Hastings was posted to Beaulieu Airfield:

> *We were billeted in huts near the airfield. When we first joined the WAAFs, our smart uniforms and doing our bit for the war effort made us feel really very proud, but in the winter when we were chipping the ice off water buckets so we could get water to wash in, we did wonder what we had let ourselves in for. Conditions when we were at Calshot were better, but looking back I am glad I was able to do my small bit despite everything.*

The use by the military of the Forest and its natural environment as a training area was significantly underpinned by many requisitioned properties and the massive construction programme. In the west of the Forest, Fordingbridge was designated by the military as Fordingbridge 4 Div. Anti-Tank Island, and was

A veteran receives recognition during an event at Beaulieu. (Beaulieu Estate)

Site plan of RAF Calshot. (Hampshire Record Office)

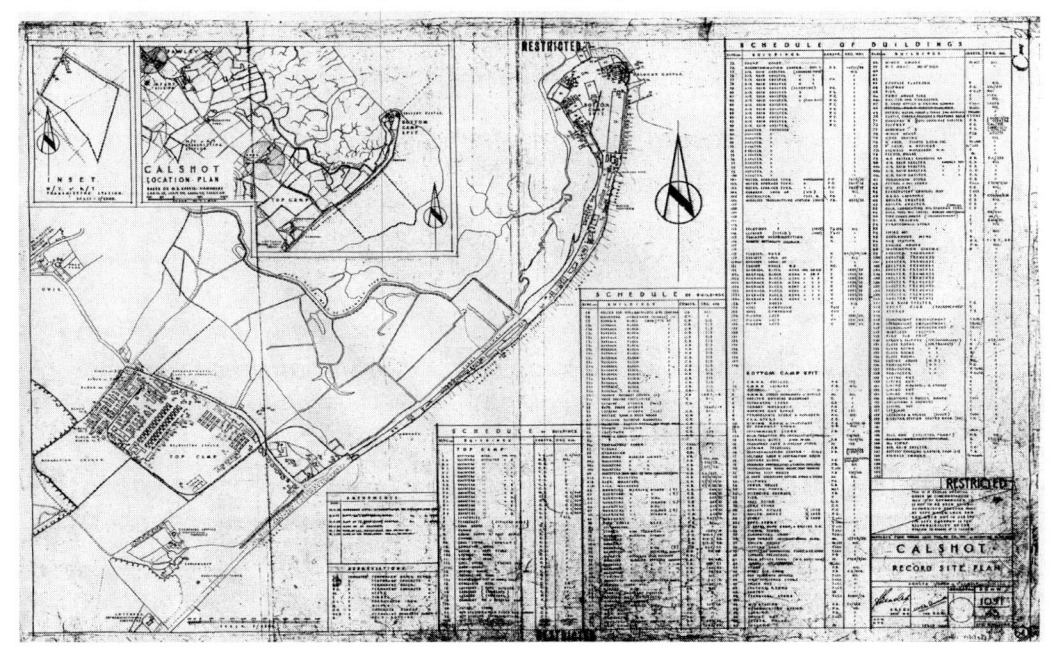

heavily fortified with thirty anti-tank barriers to which were added road blocks and trenches. A mined bridge was ready to be demolished if it was in imminent danger of being captured. The anti-tank island was part of both the General Headquarters (GHQ) line and the Southern Command, Ringwood Stop Line, which followed the River Avon from Christchurch to Salisbury via Ringwood. The Stop Line was a line of defences along main road and rail routes and waterways, built in various parts of Britain in case of a German invasion. On 14 May 1940, the war effort changed gear when the joy of an early evening radio broadcast of popular music was interrupted by an appeal by the Secretary of State for War in the new Government of Winston Churchill. In preparing for his broadcast, The Rt Hon. Anthony Eden, MP had of course been fully briefed about the sudden and effective German onslaught on Holland, Belgium, Luxembourg and France, which had taken place in the preceding days. After he had spoken about a possible enemy strike against the country by paratroopers, he raised his listeners' hope by saying that plans for repelling this strike were in place, although he could not spell out exactly what they were. Then, in his clear, resolute voice, the Secretary of State concluded his appeal:

> *Now is your opportunity. We want large numbers of such men in Great Britain who are British subjects, between the ages of seventeen and sixty-five, to come forward now and offer their service in order to make assurance doubly sure. The name of the new force, which is now to be raised, will be the Local Defence Volunteers. This name, Local Defence Volunteers, describes its duties in three words. It must be understood that this is, so to speak, a spare-time job, so there will be no need for any volunteer to abandon his present occupation. Part-time members of existing civil defence organisations should ask their officers' advice before registering under the scheme. Men who will ultimately become due for calling up under the National Service Act may join temporarily and will be released to join the army when they are required to serve.*
>
> *Now, a word to those who propose to volunteer. When on duty you will form part of the armed forces, and your period of service will be for the duration of the war. You will not be paid, but you will receive uniform*

and will be armed. You will be entrusted with certain vital duties, for which reasonable fitness and knowledge of firearms are necessary. These duties will not require you to live away from your homes. In order to volunteer, what you have to do is to give in your name at your local police station and then, as and when we want you, we will let you know.*

This appeal was directed chiefly to those who lived in small towns, villages and less densely inhabited suburban areas. It was no surprise that Hampshire and the New Forest qualified for the formation of a large number of units. Here was an opportunity for which so many had been waiting: to freely give their help and to keep the country safe.

```
CIVILIAN EMPLOYEES.
                    At the 1st June, 1944, 454 Civilian
employees viz. clerks, storemen, cleaners etc. were
employed with units.

ACCOMMODATION.
                                                            404
                Premises requisitioned number 404; those    413
hired for training 413; and those loaned free 55.            55
                                                            ———
                                                            872
CASUALTIES.  JUNE 1940 - NOVEMBER 1944.

Total number of casualties reported to
the Association............................... 972

Total number of claims to disablement
allowance...................................... 689

Total number of deaths......................... 53

CASUALTIES DUE TO ENEMY ACTION.

Killed......................................... 20

Died of wounds.................................  3

Wounded........................................ 27

NON-BATTLE CASUALTIES.

Death by injury or death from illness
contracted whilst on H.G. duty................. 30

Hospital admissions............................ 221
```

This is part of a document detailing local Home Guard manpower services. (also see overleaf). (Author's Collection)

SECRET

HAMPSHIRE DIVISION
G.S. MEMORANDA NO. 18.

477/G/1
21 Nov 41

1. **Road Blocks**

   Instructions with regard to the correct method of erecting road blocks are attached at Appx 'A'.

2. **Disposal of Students in the event of "Active Operations".**

   Instructions for the disposal of students on courses in the event of active operations are contained in W.O. letter 43/Misc/6895, sufficient copies of which were forwarded under this H.Q. letter S/471/Q dated 8 Aug 41 for distribution down to units. Further instructions on this subject dealing with students attending courses at Sn Comd schools were published in G.S. Memo No. 15 dated 14 Oct 41.

   In many instances units are failing to comply with the instructions laid down in the W.O. letter quoted above. The necessity for strict compliance with the terms of these instructions is re-emphasised, especially with regard to the details required to be forwarded with all students attending courses.

3. **Home Guard H.Q. Signs.**

   Ref G.S. Memo No. 16, para 4, dated 21 Oct 41, and G.S. Memo No. 13 para 6, dated 19 Sep 41.

   Authority is given for all Home Guard Headquarters higher than Battalions, to have a tactical sign. The sign designed for Zone Headquarters (see G.S. Memo No. 16, para 4) will be used.

4. **Damage to Property.**

   At Appx 'B' is published an Exercise Instruction issued by 1 Cdn Army Tank Bde in connection with a scheme in the NEW FOREST.

   Attention is drawn to this as being a first class example of the use of the lighter vein in putting across instructions which are apt to be treated as routine and therefore somewhat perfunctory.

5. **Pre - O.C.T.U. Training.**

   (a) R.E.

   Detailed arrangements are now completed for pre-O.C.T.U. training in a 6 weeks course at No. 2 Training Bn, R.E. of all candidates for Royal Engineers O.C.T.Us from all arms of the service.

   (b) R.A.S.C.

   Other ranks of R.A.S.C. who are recommended for commissions are to attend pre-O.C.T.U. training at R.A.S.C. Mobilisation Centre.

6. **Infantry Company Commanders School.**

   The above school situated at ANGLESEY was disbanded with effect from 27 Sep 41.

7. **Formation of an A.A. Division at Small Arms School (Hythe Wing).**

   Plans are being made to form an A.A. Division to replace the Sniper's

/Division.....

-2-

Division at the above school. With the introduction of the naval cartwheel sight it is necessary to train A.A.L.M.G. teams as specialists. It is hoped that special courses will commence in November.

8. **Change of Location - N.C.Os School R.A.S.C.**

   The above School moved from OXSHOTT to BULLER BARRACKS on 31 Aug 41.

9. **Co-operation with Police.**

   (a) Chief Constables have intimated their willingness to assist Military Schools with lectures, either on co-operation with the police or on the highway code. A lecture on co-operation is normally given at 5 Corps School, Junior Leaders Wing, each course.

   (b) This assistance will be obtained in future by direct communication between the School and the Chief Constable of the area where assistance is required.

   (c) 5 Corps School will make arrangements direct with the lecturer for the current term to repeat his lecture for future courses.

10. **C.A.P. Generator - Failures.**

    All C.A.P. generators which fail to function will in future be returned, through Ord channels, to C.O.O. TIDWORTH, who is to report on these to War Office. (Authority S.C. 6/6003/G(C") dated 23 Oct 41.)

11. **Redesignation of R.A.S.C. Units.**

    R.A.S.C. units redesignated as under will continue to carry the same serial numbers as those which were allotted to them under their previous title:

Old Designation	New Designation
20 Res M.T. Coy (98 Coy)	98 Gen Tpt Coy
21 " " " (99 Coy)	99 " " "
17 Tp Carrying Coy (225 Coy)	225 " " "
19 " " " (931 Coy)	931 " " "
20 " " " (927 Coy)	927 " " "

12. **Courses - School of Military Administration.**

    No further courses will be allotted at the above school, subsequent to the 22nd Regtl Officers Course, the 9th Corps Officers Course and the 18th N.C.Os course.

13. **Restrictions on Movement near Ordnance Depots, etc during Exercises.**

    Instances have occurred during exercises of formations harbouring in the area of an A.S.D. and causing congestion which impeded the normal flow of traffic to and from the depot. Danger to stocks was also caused by the lighting of fires and refuelling in the vicinity. During future exercises, therefore, movement near Ammunition, etc. Depots will be restricted to roads and no refuelling or lighting of fires will be permitted. Every effort should be made to park vehicles in such a way as to cause the minimum of interference with the normal traffic of the installation. Under no circumstances will troops enter the perimeter of Ordnance Dumps and factories even though these places have in theory been "captured".

    LIEUT. COLONEL. Capt
    GENERAL STAFF, HAMPSHIRE DIVISION.

Home Forces.
JOH/MJC.

A Home Guard Unit on patrol – recreated. (Nick Halling)

Whilst many veterans of the First World War, such as Ted Pickles of Totton, were very sensitive to 'general talk' of another war, they had quietly been expecting that there would be more conflict in their lifetime. Ted wrote: 'So it was with a heavy heart, true patriotism and a "do or die" resignation that we were to find ourselves once again on the "front line" albeit the front line in our own communities.'

Joy Carter, who lived near Cadnam, recalls her father saying: 'It was expected that we old 'uns would be asked to serve again. If these warmongers had been in the trenches with us first time round, we would never have had another war. I pray for all of you, my dear family.'

Those who were employed on the land had access to a gun of some sort, and if not a gun then certainly sharp and dangerous farming tools that could be used as weapons. There was a national shortage of weapons as all efforts were being directed to supplying the armed services, so an appeal for arms was duly required. From every cupboard, loft, cellar and secret hideaway came rifles, muskets and all manner of arms, many of dubious origin and many more of dubious capability. Whilst some units experienced a shortage of all the necessary items, and a newspaper quipped, 'They've got their toothbrushes, the important kit arrives next year,' initiative, improvisation and a steady flow of rifles, helmets and armbands boosted the morale of the men and of those they sought to protect.

Within just a few days of the appeal by Anthony Eden, the legal status of the LDV had been established. Detailed instructions about the organisation had been issued and some small groups of volunteers had already taken it upon themselves to patrol their neighbourhoods. By late May 1940, orders were placed in Canada for about 200,000 First World War and later pattern rifles, and these gradually filtered through to the men of the LDV in early July. But 'making do' remained at the core of the LDV's operations, and when the first rifles arrived they were distributed as fairly as possible, even though many volunteers remained ineffective soldiers because of the lack of basic equipment that it was possible to provide. Demand exceeded supply, however, because the number of volunteers had grown to three-quarters of a million men.

In mid-July Churchill made a statement in which he referred to the LDV as the 'Home Guard'. With that single comment, he raised the status of the volunteer organisation, further boosted members' morale and gave them the status they had so far lacked in the eyes of the public. When Lieutenant Colonel Thomas Moore wrote the foreword to the *Home Guard Manual 1941* in July 1940, he said: 'I am glad that the Prime Minister has indicated his desire that our name should be changed.'

Membership of the volunteer organisation by now exceeded a million men, and one unit had made the first Home Guard kill, shooting down an enemy aircraft with nothing more than rifle fire. The issue of full battledress was approved. Some units were issued with light machine guns, and as the year wore on 'making do' was replaced by 'making up' for lost time, and by improvement, heralded no doubt by the establishment of a dedicated Home Guard training centre.

The *Home Guard Manual 1941* was described in the foreword as 'a little book', although it ran to over 200 pages and was not something you could carry in the top pocket of a battledress blouse. Nonetheless it was a comprehensive, revamped version of the standard manual that had originally been issued to the Regular Army during the First World War, the giveaway being the sketches of soldiers wearing puttees.

Breamore, near Fordingbridge, had a contingent of mounted Home Guardsmen, their horses being stabled at Breamore House. The duties of these men included 'riding across the Forest looking for enemy parachutists'. On Waterside, Police Constable Kemp, who was based at Hythe police station, worked closely with the local detachment. He wrote:

> *many were veterans of the Great War, they may have seemed too old, but in fact they were ready to die for their country and they knew a trick or two to throw an enemy off balance. Because we overlook Southampton, this area was on high alert and the chaps were always out training somewhere or other in the Forest, especially on the weapons ranges at Matley Plain.*

Breamore House was used by both British and American military personnel. (Paul Raynbird)

Mounted Home Guard operated in the vicinity of Breamore House, with some horses being stabled there. (Edward Hulse)

It was not until 1943 that Noel Coward highlighted the plight of the volunteer soldiers in a song that had some home truths embedded in its whimsical lyrics. Examples of the verses include, 'Could you please oblige us with a Bren gun, or failing that, a hand grenade will do, We've got some ammunition, in a rather damp condition, And Major Huss has an arquebus that was used at Waterloo.' (An arquebus was an early muzzle-loaded firearm used between the fifteenth and seventeenth centuries.)

These selfless volunteers, despite all the jibes in the early years, proved to be a determined and reputable defence force.

9
CALLED TO ARMS

The Home Guard was the visible presence of local defence, and served as a morale booster for the public – although the debate continues to this day about its potential capabilities as an effective fighting force against an experienced enemy.

There is no doubt, however, that the Home Guard would have made its presence felt, as would another force. However, this latter force was much less well known; indeed, its very existence was on a need-to-know basis and few needed to know, including family members. Britain's 'secret army', also known as Churchill's secret army and Churchill's guerrilla army, comprised some 4,000 men, all courageous volunteers who were prepared from the outset to sacrifice their lives if a German invasion of Britain took place. Formed into units or cells across the country and issued with top secret orders, if church bells rang to warn of enemy invasion the Auxiliary Unit (AU) volunteers were to disappear without telling anyone and report to hidden bases in the countryside. Every man was issued with sealed orders (other organisations including the NFS were also issued with secret orders) to be opened only in the event of an invasion, and these included a list of potential collaborators. This included people as senior as chief constables and Justices of the Peace as well as some rank-and-file police officers. Intelligence sources in the German-occupied Channel Islands had reported that police officers had been susceptible to collaboration, and the British government had no intention of a repeat of this in mainland Britain. Simply put, collaborators might have to be executed if there was a risk of them helping the enemy. Interestingly, chief constables were responsible for the Home Guard in some areas of the country, and most police stations had an arms

An Auxiliary Unit photographed during a local training session. (CART)

cabinet as well as a pistol within easy reach of the duty sergeant.

Most of the AU volunteers worked in the countryside and were specifically selected for their local knowledge, their country skills (hunting, for example) and the ability to use a weapon. The men, who were trained at Coleshill in the Vale of the White Horse, Oxfordshire, operated in small groups from disguised bases, which were often underground. Some of these bases remain hidden to this day, not least because they were so well hidden and many volunteers took the knowledge of the locations to the grave. Their role was to disrupt and destroy the enemy's supply chain, to kill collaborators and to take out strategic targets, and because they were unable to tell anyone about their activities they had to disguise their true activities. More often than not, members did this by pretending to belong to the Home Guard, which explains why in post-war years these units have often been incorrectly referred to as the Home Guard Auxiliary.

Here, then, in remembrance of the AU members from the New Forest, is information about the clandestine patrols upon whose services the nation would have called in the event of invasion.

Avon Castle Patrol (inauguration date unknown)

This patrol was part of Group 1 in Hampshire which was commanded by Captain A.J. Champion, also Area Commander (AC) for all the West Hampshire groups. The Assistant Commander (AAC) of Group 1 was Lieutenant L.D.C. Ayles.

Name	Date of Birth	Occupation		Died
Sgt Sydney Leonard Moss	26/08/1893	Antiques		1980
Pte G.E. Jones	27/07/1904			
Pte J.A. Frampton	03/12/1899			
Pte Albert George Frampton	18/08/1909		Joined HM Forces May 1943	1976
Bertie D. Brumwell	26/07/1922		Joined HM Forces April 1943	
Frederick W. Canning	27/10/1922		Joined HM Forces April 1943	
Wallace W. Dyson	10/06/1913		Joined HM Forces April 1943	
Wallace W Dyson returned to Unit June 1943			Re-joined HM Forces June 1944	
H.A. Green	12/02/1909		Joined HM Forces April 1943	
Peter Thomas Parkin	03/01/1924		Joined HM Forces Sept. 1943	
A.F. Wiseman	10/06/1916		Joined HM Forces April 1943	

Spetisbury Auxiliary Unit in the neighbouring county of Dorset. (CART)

The patrol names for the west of Hampshire and the New Forest have been identified from National Archives file, WO199/3391, but are not divided by patrol. The nominal roll gives the surname, initials, Identity Card (ID) number and address, together with date of birth. The patrols have been arranged according to the addresses and ID card numbers around known patrol leaders. This means the allocations may not be completely accurate. Some men, particularly those from the Ringwood area where there were several patrols, could not be allocated with any confidence to one patrol or another, so are listed here.

Sydney Moss was an antique dealer from London who moved to Avon Castle in Ringwood during the war. He was promoted to second lieutenant in July 1944 and full lieutenant in August of the same year. G.E. Jones is also said to have lived at Avon Castle, although it is thought the accommodation address given was a timber merchant's offices, part of which was rented out.

In the nominal roll, addresses are normally rubbed out, having been written in pencil in case of changes when men leave the unit. However, parts of the original address are often still visible and these, together with the ID card numbers, which include a geographic code and the position in the register, which appears to have been completed in unit order, allows patrol allocations to be made. In this case it appears that a large part of the patrol went into the forces together. It can be speculated that this was because they shared a common occupation, which ceased to be exempt from call up, particularly since they are of different ages. Given that all appear to have had an Avon Castle address, perhaps they all worked in the timber trade.

Brockenhurst Patrol (inauguration date unknown)
This was part of Group 2 in Hampshire, commanded by Lieutenant G.B. Ash. The AAC of Group 2 was Lieutenant G. Forward.

Name	Date of Birth	Occupation		Died
Sgt John James C.K. Slightam	29/03/1894			
Pte Harry J Burt	04/04/1925	Forester		1994
Pte Harold Frank Emm	13/06/1899			
Pte A.E. Fisher	04/08/1911		Probably Arthur	
Pte R.J. Wells	12/02/1921			
Pte J. Moseley	14/11/1910		Posted 3rd Bn HG May 1944	
Pte Arthur Eric R. Warr	23/02/1921		'Casualty' October 1942	1975

Harry Burt lived in a forester's cottage at South Weirs. Arthur Warr is listed as a casualty and left the unit in October 1942. However, 'casualty' is a military term and it does not necessarily mean that he was injured in any way. While

105

most other transfers and departures are given details, this has no details at all. Nothing more is known about the other men in this patrol other than they all resided in the Brockenhurst area.

Burley Patrol (inauguration date unknown)

The patrol was part of Group 1 in Hampshire; it was commanded by Captain A.J. Champion. The AAC of Group 1 was Lieutenant L.D.C. Ayles.

Name	Date of Birth	Occupation		Died
Sgt John William Shutler	09/06/1891	Garage owner	Possibly ASC First World War	1968
Pte F.W. King	04/09/1899			
Pte Walter John Marchant	03/08/1893	Gardener	Joined September 1942	1959
Pte F.T. Rolfe	23/01/1897		Joined March 1943	
Pte Edward Hartley Summerell	09/06/1902		Joined September 1942	1987
Pte Frank F. Finch	16/11/1890		Joined June 1943	
Pte Frederick William Carpenter	03/06/1900			

The Burley patrol members were older than the average age of the members of the other Auxiliary Units because all of them had fought in the First World War. Jack Shutler ran the garage on Burley Street and his two brothers also worked in the village, one with a garage and the other at the livery stables. A number of the men listed joined later, according to the AU nominal roll. While sometimes this can be inaccurate, it does suggest that there were other men who formed part of the patrol prior to this, yet their details have not been recorded.

Shortly after the war, Brian Marchant was taken by his father, Walter, to see the Operational Base (OB) in woods just outside Burley. He describes a hidden hatch, with steps down to a fair-sized room with wooden bunks and a table. Forestry Commission employee Ken Harding recalls being asked to take his digger and excavate and destroy the bunker. It was constructed of steel sheets and was quite substantial, taking a significant effort to break it up and bury it completely.

Cadnam Patrol (inauguration date unknown)
The patrol was part of Group 2 in Hampshire, and was commanded by Lieutenant G.B. Ash.

Name	Date of Birth	Occupation		Died
Sgt Henry Rebbeck Green	31/03/1897			1969
Pte Bert Corbidge	18/06/1912			1967
Pte Harold John Crouch	02/07/1912			1985
Pte William Charles May	07/01/1898			1980
Pte Mark George Quinton	08/12/1897			1953
Pte George Ernest W. Smith	31/10/1906			
Pte Arthur Thomas Walker	18/04/1910			

Some men, particularly those from the Ringwood area where there were several patrols, cannot be allocated with any confidence to one patrol or another.

Fordingbridge Patrol (inauguration date unknown)

The patrol was part of Group 1 in Hampshire, commanded by Captain A.J. Champion.

Name	Date of Birth	Occupation		Died
Sgt Albert Chafen Broad	09/12/1889			1957
Pte G.B. Bowles	04/07/1913			1989
Pte Reginald John Fry	04/01/1906			2003
Pte H.E. Harper	06/10/1890			
Pte Frederick Charles Molloy	13/09/1909			1988
Pte A.J. Rogers	30/11/1913			
Pte Edward 'Ted' Rogers	06/08/1923		Joined HM Forces Jan. 1943	2005
Pte Samson L.J. Wells	26/02/1897			
Pte R.F. Young	09/10/1896			

The Fordingbridge patrol comprised men who lived to the north and west of the Avon Valley area. There was another patrol in another group on the other side of the river, around the area of Hale.

Reginald Fry came from Weymouth, where he had married the daughter of a Church of Scotland minister before the war. He was there when issued with his ID card: the Weymouth code indicates he was a resident in 1939. Returning there after the war, his death was recorded in the town.

The Rogers both lived at the same address, and therefore are likely to have been brothers.

Fritham Patrol (inauguration early 1940)

The patrol was part of Group 2 in Hampshire, commanded by Lieutenant Ash. Captain Champion was the AC for all the West Hampshire groups.

Name	Date of Birth	Occupation		Died
Sgt Bertie Benjamin Smith	24/01/1904	Forester	Took over from G. Forward	1966
Pte William Charles Gulliver	28/8/1899	Forester		
Pte W. Thorne	19/08/1900	Forest worker		
Pte Allister Thomas Holloway	17/12/1902	Forest keeper		1967
Pte A.H. Holland	12/02/1912		Joined HM Forces May 1944	
Pte Charles Albert Peckham	11/10/1896		Posted to 8th Bn HG	

The Fritham Patrol was started by Gerald Forward, who was almost certainly the patrol's sergeant from its creation until he was promoted to Assistant Group Commander in April 1944. He later recounted some of the details of this time in a privately published autobiography. Gerald was an agister (who assisted with the management of the stock owned by the commoners of the Forest) with specific responsibility for the welfare of free-ranging animals, and with his brother Hubert covered the 93,000 acres of the Forest during the war. He recalled how he was initially approached by a staff officer, who circled the subject at some length before asking him to find the men to form a patrol. This was apparently quite early on in the war, possibly July to September 1940, and certainly after the renaming of the LDV on 22 July 1940.

Bertie Smith, Bill Gulliver and Allister Holloway all occupied well-known foresters' cottages in the Forest (Holly Hatch, Bramshaw Wood and Coppice of Linwood respectively). These were official residences that came with the job

The ER Brockadale Auxiliary Patrol re-enactors recreate a wartime scene in an Auxiliary Unit hideout. (CART)

and formed part of the unique structure of the New Forest. It is likely that the rest of the patrol were in similar occupations.

One of the patrol's OBs was a caravan that had been completely buried, with a disguised entrance and in 'a part of the Forest which was difficult to get to'. This caravan belonged to the Crosthwaite-Eyre family, well known in the New Forest, with various members of the family representing the area as MP, as Official Verderer (the verderer's role being to protect and administer the unique agricultural commoning practices in the Forest) and during the war as commander of the local Home Guard. Gerald Forward spoke to John Crosthwaite-Eyre, whom he knew was involved in similar work – although it is not clear if he knew how much (John was pictured at Coleshill House at this time) – and one afternoon the caravan was carefully hitched to a tractor and driven off, after John's staff had gone to lunch. It was buried by the following morning.

The patrol also had a more typical corrugated iron shelter, the wood for this being acquired from one of the Forest bridges! This is thought to have been in Bramshaw Wood but no longer exists, as it was dug up by Gerald Forward for use as a pigsty after the war. Gerald reports that the AU trained with regular soldiers, possibly a Hampshire Scout Section, as well as being sent on a training course; it is most likely that this was a patrol leader's course at Coleshill House.

Just prior to the caravan episode, Gerald Forward and John Crosthwaite-Eyre made their own grenades. It is probable that this was when the Home Guard had little more than Molotov cocktails and shotguns. These grenades were made of cement contained within brown paper and filled with metal debris such as nails and tacks, with a piece of cord as the detonator. Gerald remarked that these were probably most dangerous to the user! A cache of them was discovered after the war at The Warrens, the Crosthwaite-Eyre residence, and the police were called since it was not immediately apparent why they were there.

After the war, Gerald Forward was elected as a verderer, and was awarded an MBE for this work in the 1974 New Year's Honours list.

Lyndhurst Patrol (inauguration early 1940)

This was part of Group 2 in Hampshire, commanded by Lieutenant Ash with Captain Champion as the AC. The AAC was Lieutenant Forward.

Name	Date of Birth	Occupation		Died
Sgt J.H. Adams	03/02/1894	Forester		
Pte George Ben Broomfield	28/02/1904	Forester		1981
Pte Henry Charles Barnes	18/08/1892			

Pte Frederick C. Core	07/08/1880			1946
Pte Edward Augustus Soffe	31/08/1901			1965
Pte E.H.S. Wilson	03/04/1919			
Pte J. Collins	29/03/1895			
Pte Lionel Benjamin Wren	29/6/1888	Keeper	Posted to 9th Bn HG Jan. 1943	1948

Sergeant Adams and George Broomfield both lived in foresters' cottages, Denny Lodge and Lodge Hill respectively, so they were most likely to have been employed in that role. Lionel Wren was a keeper, an official appointment that merited a mention in the *London Gazette* in 1936.

Ringwood 1 Patrol (inauguration date unknown)

The patrol was part of Group 1 in Hampshire, commanded by Captain Champion, with the assistant commander being Lieutenant Ayles. The Probert family remember both Champion and Ayles being involved.

Name	Date of Birth	Occupation		Died
Sgt Leslie Charles 'Elsie' Probert	16/11/1900	Butcher		1988
Pte John Rutland Probert	06/07/1923	Butcher's assistant	Joined August 1941	1967
Pte R. Pritchard	15/05/1911		Joined June 1943	
Pte William S. Stephenson	02/10/1904		Joined April 1942	
Pte William Charles Crutcher	09/10/1906		Joined June 1942	1980

Leslie 'Elsie' Probert was a butcher with a shop on Southampton Road, Ringwood, alongside Woolworth's and with a pillbox outside. Leslie's nickname came from the sound of his initials. Some of the patrol's supplies were reportedly kept at the butcher's shop where the family lived for the early part of the war. These included the rum jar, which was dropped and smashed by Leslie's fourteen-year-old son, Peter, who remembers the trouble he got into! John Probert was almost certainly Leslie's eldest son, who helped out in the shop and joined the unit when he reached the age of eighteen. He was not eligible for call up, apparently because he had flat feet, so he served with the AU instead. John was usually in charge of the shop as Leslie, who was also a meat agent for the Ministry of Food, spent much of his time travelling all over Hampshire, including the Isle of Wight. Both father and son seem to have been quite secretive about what they were up to and rarely mentioned it, even after the war, and then only in vague terms. It was said that a requirement of AU membership was the ability to swim the river in full kit. This surprised Leslie's children, who did not think he could have managed this.

Bill Stephenson was the local chemist. His shop was three doors down from the Proberts' butcher's shop.

R. Pritchard is not known for certain to have been a member of the patrol, but in the nominal roll his address has been switched with John Probert's, their names being next to each other in the handwritten roll. This suggests they were in the same unit, as the men seem to have been added to each alphabetical page in unit order.

William Charles Crutcher is not remembered by the Probert family by name, but Mary remembers an incident where one of the patrol members was accidentally shot in the foot while in the OB. Her mother was not best pleased that a man had been hurt and said they were nothing more than stupid schoolboys! William Crutcher put in a claim after the war for a disability pension, something he could only have done if he had been injured during training.

There was an underground bunker in the vicinity of Hangersley Hill, which Leslie's daughter learnt about when she was confronted at the breakfast table one morning. Her father had seen her in the area with a soldier the previous night while he was training at the OB, and he took her to task over the matter.

Peter Probert recalls that there was also an underground bunker in the woods near Somerley House. It is known that there was a unit there, so the men may have trained together.

Patrol targets are likely to have included the airfield at Ibsley. The patrol is known to have trained at Avon Castle, as did other local patrols. The Proberts are known to have had revolvers and a knuckleduster, as they took these home. Detonators, hand grenades and ammunition were stored in a garage near their house. They also used thunder flashes in training.

Bill Stephenson became a president of Ringwood Rotary Club after the war, an honour also achieved by three other members of AUs from the Ringwood area: Ray Withall, Ted Geary and Ted Harvey.

Ringwood 2 Patrol (inauguration date unknown)
This patrol was commanded by Captain Champion.

Name	Date of Birth	Occupation		Died
Sgt Arthur Charles Hoskins	29/09/1911		Joined May 1942	1951
Pte Edward Ernest Geary	01/03/1909			1995
Pte Frederick Samuel Geary	20/12/1904			1972
Pte Clarence Jack L. Hanham	20/04/1905		Joined June 1942, known as Jack	1976
Pte George P. Gale	11/04/1911		Joined Sept. 1943	
Pte Raymond Alfred R. Withall	29/09/1911			1980

Fred Geary worked in the family butcher's and grocer's shop; Ted Geary was his brother. At the start of the war he was just over the age for call up, and he is said to have had a minor heart attack as well, so he joined the LDV. He didn't speak of his involvement in AUs, but talked about having been in the Home Guard. June Bentley, his daughter, recalls that he enjoyed going out 'with the lads' training on a Sunday morning, although they usually ended up in the pub, drinking or playing darts. He told tales of how on exercises they had captured another platoon, or been captured themselves. But, of course, it was never his fault.

George Gale had moved from Dorset, having probably been a member of a patrol there, possibly Moreton. He is recorded as leaving in January 1942 at his own request, but he did not rejoin in Hampshire until September 1943. Unusually, therefore, it appears he served in two AU patrols in two different counties.

David Hoskins, the son of Arthur Charles Hopkins, has his father's papers, which include ID cards that show him as both a member of the OC and also the ARP Rescue Party leader at different times. He is listed as joining in mid-1942, yet became patrol leader quite quickly, and had a copy of the usual stand down letter that was issued by AUs in November 1944. David recalled that his father served with Fred Geary, Jack Hanham and George Gale. It has been assumed that Fred's brother Ted and his very near neighbour Ray Withall were also in this patrol.

It is thought that the OB was located near Three Tree Hill on the outskirts of Ringwood, in the Highwood and Moyle's Court area. Nearby Ibsley airfield would have been a very likely patrol target.

The patrol was training at Avon Castle on one occasion when a German bomber was shot down and crash landed in the meadows close by. According to records, this is likely to have been a Junkers JU88A-4 of 2/KG6, which crashed at Southmead Meadows, near Westover Farm, on 7 May 1943. The patrol also met to train on Fred Geary's 8-acre field just outside Ringwood, close to Moyle's Court. Arthur Hoskins attended at least one patrol leaders' course at Coleshill. The timetable includes the names of Major Oxenden and Captain Delamere, dating this to 1942 or later, as these officers were elsewhere before this.

St Leonards Hotel, Ringwood, in the garden of which was discovered an Auxiliary Unit radio monitoring station. (Olde English Inns)

David Hoskins recalled his father had weapons and ammunition in their larder, and behind paint tins on the top shelf of the garden shed were boxes of grenades, time pencils and tripwires.

After the war, Fred Geary demonstrated his explosives training on occasion. His daughter remembers a large hole being blown in the lawn one fireworks night as he set off some left-over detonators. His son recalls seeing one or more hand grenades in a drum of oil in the workshop (soaking in oil is one way in which to deactivate cordite).

Ringwood 3 Patrol (inauguration date unknown)
The patrol was commanded by Captain A.J. Champion; AAC of Group 1 was Lieutenant Ayles.

Name	Date of Birth	Occupation		Died
Sgt. Joseph Maitland Roger	24/06/1912			1991

Only the patrol leader is known for this patrol. There were other members, but the home addresses overlap with those of the Ringwood 2 Patrol, making it difficult to know which men were in which unit. Unusually, the patrol leader appears only to have joined the Home Guard in July 1942, so it may be that there was someone else before him. Since both Captain Champion and Lieutenant Ayles came from Ringwood, it is possible that one of them originally commanded this unit.

Ringwood 'C' Patrol (inauguration date unknown)
The patrol was part of Group 1 in Hampshire, commanded by Captain Champion.

Name	Date of Birth	Occupation		Died
Sgt Joseph Maitland Roger	24/06/1912			1991

All the comments for Ringwood 3 Patrol are applicable.

Somerley Patrol (inauguration date unknown)
The patrol was part of Group 1 in Hampshire.

Name	Date of Birth	Occupation		Died
CSM John Harry Burrett	17/04/1908			1969
Pte Arthur William Hudspith	21/04/1910			2002

Pte William Alexander Rabbets	01/10/1909			1985
Pte R.B. Rowson	23/02/1906		Joined Feb. 1943	
Pte F. Warwick	14/8/1888		posted to 8th Bn Hants HG Dec. 1942	
Pte S.W. Warwick	11/09/1921		joined Gren. Guards Mar. 1943	
Pte Vivian John Debben	09/10/1928			2004
Pte E. Rands	07/08/1896			
Pte N.H.M. Jones	12/02/1896		posted to 8th Bn Hants HG Mar. 1943	

All the men listed here were living on the Somerley Estate near Ringwood or nearby at Blashford. It is likely that there were other patrol members who have not yet been identified. Company Sergeant Major (CSM) Burrett would probably have been involved in the administration of the West Hampshire AUs, but was still listed as the patrol commander soon before the end of the war.

In the 1980s, an underground bunker typical of the type used for an AU OB, was found on the former RAF Ibsley site, which was part of the Somerley Estate. This base has subsequently been destroyed by gravel extraction. Airfield construction did not start until late in 1940, and it is possible that the OB was in place before it was known that the airfield was to be built; there were other defensive anti-aircraft gun-sites nearby.

It is likely that a second OB was built elsewhere on the estate. There are reports from other Ringwood patrols about an underground base on the

Somerley Estate. Many OBs had concealed entrances that were secured with various locks, catches and 'booby traps'.

West of Hampshire and the New Forest

Patrol names for this area have been identified from National Archives file WO199/3391, but are not divided by patrol. The nominal roll gives the surname, initials, ID card number and address, together with date of birth. The patrols have been arranged, according to the addresses and ID card numbers, around known patrol leaders. This means the allocations may not be completely accurate. Additional personal information such as first names and dates of death have been added using the 1911 census, Ancestry.co.uk and FreeBMD. com. Some men, particularly those from the Ringwood area where there are several patrols, could not be allocated with any confidence to one patrol or another.

Patrol locality and members' names:

Name	Date of Birth		Died
Pte Ronald J. Gardner	20/06/1915		1997
Pte W.J. Lewis	13/07/1902		
Pte J. Mitchell	18/7/1899	Transferred July 1944	
Pte Maurice William Pelling	12/10/1910	Joined HM Forces, April 1943	1975
Pte A.J. Coward	26/09/1904		
Pte Robert Plenderleith	13/09/1911		1983

Pte Albert Edward Cobb	14/08/1902	left c.1942	
Pte Richard Attwood	20/7/1896	Posted 8th Bn Hants HG May 1943	
Pte Bryan Herbert S. Guy	12/12/1913	Nurseryman	1997

 J. Mitchell was transferred to Devon Auxiliary Units when he moved to Newton Abbot in July 1944. Bryan Guy was a nurseryman at Belle Vue Nurseries in Ringwood, which still operates today. His daughter was friends with Mary Probert, daughter of Ringwood A's patrol leader, but she is fairly certain he was not serving with her father. If you have any information regarding the above named, please contact the team at Coleshill.

Fortunately, AU members were never called upon, yet they trained and were ready for the day when invasion might come. At a moment's notice they would have been able to face an tried and tested enemy. As the enemy fought to gain ground, the AUs would have engaged in such ruthless tactics as were necessary to protect their territory, with the advantages of determination and surprise on their side.
 It is only in recent years that the AUs have started to gain recognition for their place in the nation's wartime history, although many records and details of precise roles remain embargoed until the year 2045.

10
A Day in the Life

The USAAF (United States Army Air Force) flew both fighters and bombers from airfields in the Forest. Here are extracts from the unit logs from Winkton airfield.

Headquarters 404th Fighter Bomber Group
Station 414 (Winkton) England

SECTION I
1 Organisation: Negative
2. Strength:
A Officers 30
B. Enlisted men 80
3. Date of arrival and departure from each station in the ETO: Arrived at station 414 on 4th April 1944 and remained there
4. Awards to and decorations of the unit: Negative

SECTION II TRAINING
During the month of May all pilots received non-operational training in Homing Dive Bombing Group Formations and cloud flying. In addition to the Operational Training, all pilots received extended Intelligence Training in Aircraft Recognition, Tank Recognition, Geography, Air Sea Rescue, Map Reading, Methods of Escape and Evasion. The highlight of the Intelligence Training was a 3-hour lecture on Flak by Major Brett of the R.A.F. who discussed to great extent the possibility of being hit

by flak and also the difference between light and heavy flak. During the month, the enlisted men went through a waterproofing exercise whereby personnel of all sections who drive or who was an assistant driver were given instructions on how to waterproof a vehicle, and at the close of the instruction, all the personnel drove the vehicle through the wading pond; with the exception of wet pants and shoes all came through with flying colours.

Throughout the month of May various officers and enlisted men continued to be sent to schools in the ETO for further training.

SECTION III OPERATIONS
The Group became operational on the 1st day of May 1944 and during the month flew 23 missions, which consisted of Fighter Sweeps, Escorting Medium and Heavy Bombers, and Dive Bombing. Generally speaking, very little Enemy Fighter opposition was encountered on any of these missions however, they did meet up with a bit on 19 May while on a dive bombing mission led by the Group Deputy Commander Major Johnson when they encountered 6 ME-109s just NT of Rouser. The enemy aircraft broke to the left and pulled up in split-dive and 1st Lt. Ben Kitchen of the 508th squadron followed through one of the enemy aircraft aft and destroyed it. Again, on May 24th while on an escort mission 9 FW 190s followed the Group approximately 2000 feet above the escort and to the rear, but made no attempt to attack or engage the escort. During the same mission while seeking to provide cover for straggling bombers, our planes were fired upon three times by the bombers. Light to heavy flak was encountered on several missions however all pilots returned safely from all the missions with only slight damage to a couple of planes.

During this month, the pilots received their christening of combat flying and all in all they came through with flying colours.

SECTION IV – ADMINISTRATION
In the month of May, promotions of great interest were made in this

Group. The first was the promotion of the Group Deputy Commander, Major James K. Johnson to Lt. Colonel on May 20 1944. The second promotion came on May 25th when our Group Commander Lt. Colonel Carroll W. McColpin was promoted to the rank of full Colonel. Both of these promotions were received with great enthusiasm throughout the Group.

SECTION V – RECREATION
Under the able guidance of 1st Lt. 'Dyke' Pisegna of the Special Services, the Athletic program has progressed so much that there isn't an evening that passes when there isn't a sport contest of some form or other taking place. Softball has held the spotlight for the 404th for the past two weeks and a synopsis of the present standing follows:

SCORES OF GROUP SOFTBALL GAMES

Group HQ Officers	2
506th Sqdn Officers	7
Group HQ Officers	5
507th Sqdn Officers	11
Group HQ Enlisted Men	0
506th Sqdn Enlisted Men	9
Group HQ Enlisted Men	6
507th Sqdn Enlisted Men	0
Group HQ Enlisted Men	4
507th Sqdn Enlisted Men	6

Capt. 'Buck' Buckberry of Special Services and Capt. 'Dud' Connor of S-2 filled the positions of pitcher and catcher respectively. The four outstanding hitters for the Group Officers were Lt. Col. Johnson with an average of .666, Lt. Pisegna with .664, Capt. Buckberry with .595 and Lt. Marshall with .542; it is also noted that Lt. Pell bats. The Rising Star, Boy to be watched, Man Going Forward, is our own weather man, 2nd Lt. Ted Crosthwait, who is playing a bang-up game at center field. Athletic games thus far have been played on the Group's own 'McGook' field.

The Volley Ball games have also been very popular this past month with the Group Officers taking over the Group Enlisted men at two different times in the best out of 3. However, the Group Officers were taken over by the 506th Sqdn Enlisted men in the best 2 out of 3.

Thanks to Lt. Pisegna, the 404th is now well equipped with sports facilities. At the present time, we have 6 volley ball courts, 4 softball diamonds, 1 outdoor basketball court, and 1 horseshoe pit. In addition, a softball and volleyball league is being organised and many heated contests are in the offering for the future.

SECTION VI – NOTES OF SPECIAL INTEREST
On May 25th, we were honoured by the unexpected visit of Major General Brereton, the Commanding General of the Ninth Air Force. The 404th Enlisted Men's Glee Club went on a tour to Ascot and gave two concerts to the officers and enlisted men of the Ninth Air Force on May 26th and 27th. The concert for the enlisted men was presented at the Arrow Club and the one for the officers was presented at the General's dance at the Berkshire Club. At both performances great applause was given and the boys were called back for several encores.

506th Fighter Bomber Squadron
404th Fighter Bomber Group
Station 414
England
Unit history for the month of May 1944
2nd Lt. Melvin H Johnson
Air Corps Historical Officer
10 June 44

A P47 aircraft of 404 Group USAAF based at Winkton. (John Leavesley)

Organisation: Negative

Strength: As of the first day of May this squadron had 50 officers and 251 enlisted men for a total of 301.

Date of Arrival and departure in the European Theatre of Operations (ETO): Negative.

Losses in action: 1st Lt. Charles P. Clonts, 0794204, was hit by a Messerschmidt [sic] ME109 and/or flak [flieger abwehr kanone, German anti-aircraft fire] over Soissons 8 May 1944. He was seen to go down in smoke. Now carried as Missing in Action (MIA). On 9 May within a 10 mile inland radius of Dieppe, on the route home, 2nd Lt. Joseph C Joyce JR, 0677947, was heard to say that he was bailing out. Lt. Joyce's ship had been hit by flak over the target, which was construction works at

Serqueux. It was believed that his oil line had been damaged, for he had been able to stay with the squadron to the area mentioned. Now carried as MIA.

Wounded: 1st Lt. Harvey P. Bates, 0796065, while on a dive bombing mission, 22 May 1944, received a slight wound in his right leg. While diving on the target, which was a roundhouse [locomotive shed] at Bethune, a 20mm anti-aircraft shell exploded inside his cockpit. Lt. Bates 'heard the music' on this one – the map case just to his right was damaged beyond all repair.

Awards: Negative

Part played in war effort:
On 1 May 1944, the group became operational and this squadron flew two missions. During the entire month 20 missions were flown for a total of 304 sorties and constituted five fighter sweeps, six dive bombings and nine escorts. Briefings for missions were held in the Group briefing room. Squadron intelligence officers took turns at giving the facts to the pilots before take-off. Interrogations were handled by the squadron itself. The situation map was placed in the pilots' snack bar and although interrogations [debriefings] were a bit pressed for space, the set up proved quite successful. Major Harold G Shook, Commanding Officer, won top honours in missions flown by participating in all flights.

The squadron experienced its first victory during this month. 2nd Lt. Chester L. Dunmore, 0725696, while engaging in a fighter sweep on 8 May, shot down an ME 109. The encounter lasted approximately one minute and took place in the vicinity of Soissons. Six ME109s attacked the flight from above at 5 o'clock and it was here that Lt. Clonts was shot down. Lt. Dunsmore immediately followed up the attack on Lt. Clonts. He observed his hits on the enemy plane and smoke was seen to stream from the German ship. Bits of the plane flew off. Official confirmation of this claim has not yet been received from higher headquarters.

2nd Lt. Harry E. Anderson, 0689730, thought he was experiencing *a case of the 'DTs' when on a mission, he observed two ships flying in perfect formation except for one small detail – the lead ship was flying upside down and the other plane right side up. It seems as though they were just breaking through the cloud and the upside-down pilot was suffering from a bad attack of vertigo. For a short minute, Lt. Anderson thought he was the pilot gone temporarily berserk, but a quick check told him he was flying in the conventional manner – that is, right side up. Lt. Anderson had difficulty in making others believe his story until the abortive came in with the verdict of vertigo.*

Lt. George W. Stovall, 0671798, returning from a mission over France, told the interrogating officer that the flak was so thick that he could have dropped his wheels and taxied on it. The tail assembly of his ship suffered about 20 flak holes, which he used to back up his statement.

Human Interest:
During off hours, softball became the squadron's pastime. Enlisted men and officers had several games. During these contests the excitement and lust of battle ran high. War was forgotten and the final score was uppermost in the players' and spectators' minds. Cheering and razzing went hand in hand as the games progressed. Good humoured boos and cat calls were many when the lowly umpire had to pass judgement on a close play. Officers games between the other squadrons and group were always hotly contested.

A pilot's snack bar was made with a glider crate and an ammunition blister. Interrogations were held there. Lounging chairs and sofas were procured while the kitchen was composed of refrigerator and a small stove. Hot coffee, warm Spam sandwiches, eggs and oranges greeted pilots as they came in from cold missions.

Unit History – 507th Fighter Bomber Squadron
Instalment for 1–31 May 1944

Andrew F Wilson Capt Air Corps Historical Officer
12 June 44

Organisation:
To take the place of 1st Lieut. Robert DeGregorio, transferred to Group headquarters, and to fill the vacancy created by the new T.O. [Table of Organisation], two new engineering officers were assigned to the squadron during the month, 2nd Lieut. James S. O'Connor and 2nd Lieut. John F. Volker. [1st Lieutenant DeGregorio's success in 'organising' the underwing fitments for the 507th was not, it appears, overlooked by Group, who obviously considered his considerable skill should be exploited for the good of the Group as a whole – John Levesley].

Six new pilots were assigned, 2nd Lieuts Donald M. Ferris, James F. Hall, John J. Rodgers Jr, Edgar E. Grove and John F. Phelps.

Among the enlisted men there were 14 promotions during the month, dispelling the rumour that promotions are slow in the ETO.

Strength:
As of 31 May the squadron had 50 officers and 251 enlisted men.

Movement, Casualties and Decorations – negative

Narrative:
On 1 May, this squadron together with the rest of the 404th Group went operational. By the end of the month the pilots had flown 22 missions totalling 58 hours, averaging 2 hours and 40 minutes per mission. They made 342 sorties and ran up 850 total operational flying hours without serious loss or serious damage by enemy action.

By the end of May, 10 men had become eligible for the Air Medal with one oak leaf cluster and 21 others for the Air Medal. Capt. Charles C. 'Lad' Lutman was the first in the outfit to be recommended for the medal getting his 9th and 10th sortie credits on 9 May. Cluster winners included our C.O. Major Clay Tice Jr. who earned two oak leaves to add to his Southwest Pacific award, Capt Howard L. Galbreath, operations officer, Capt. Lutman, First Lieutenants Robert W. Green, Duane D. Int-Hout, Stephen V. Leonard, John C. Ross, Thomas L. Weller and Benjamin F. Yeargin Jr., and Second Lieutenant Russell S. Fredendall.

Nine missions were bomber escort, five were fighter sweeps, four were dive-bombing, three were covering dive-bombing by the rest of the group, and one was a sweep forced back by weather from the French coast.

The curious thing about every mission flown during the month was the feeling you got during the planning phase. 'Hope to hell they all get back but they just can't miss running into some fireworks this time.' But only one ship was even damaged by flak. Capt. Lutman picked up a small hole in his wing surface near Nielun aerodrome, south east of Paris, on a deep fighter sweep on 8 May. And there were no engagements with enemy aircraft; only two sightings, Me 209s at great range Southeast of Paris on 8 May and a few MEs and FWs near Beauvais on 19 May while on a dive bomber escort.

The first mission was just a shallow penetration sweep 40 miles inland over Normandy. By 31 May, spares and aborts were sticking with the formation to more remote and dangerous areas than that, but May 1 was important and exciting. This was IT. The briefing at group took at least 20 minutes, the intelligence officer showing all his pictures of landfalls in and out through the balopticon, the weather officer projected his weather charts on the screen, the group CO, Lt. Col. Carroll W. McColpin carefully covered the take-off; formation procedure and flak evasion. And at the subsequent critique, the Colonel, all smiles, had to caution the gang about over evasiveness.

According to Second Lieutenant Russell S. 'Freddie' Fredenhall, 'When we crossed that French coast, the sawdust really hit the fan. One minute we were flying along in perfect formation and the next minute there were planes all over the sky. We were trying to throw the enemy predictors off before the guns opened fire – like the Colonel told us! No we never did see any flak.'

The course home brought the squadron back right over Carpiquet airdrome at 20,000 feet. The Colonel seemed surprised when no one else reported the two FW 190s four miles straight down in the corner of the field.

As the month passed, with the 506th and the 508th each being bounced once apiece by MEs while the 507th flying the same missions in the same area was unmolested, we all began feeling with increased confidence that our good tight formations were keeping Jerry away. As it was the previous month on training flights our formations were good to the point of distinguishing the squadron from the others in the air.

Our only bad scares and narrow escapes happened on this side of the channel – all on take-off. Worst was the accident to Capt. Ray C. Langford on 11 May. He was taking off on an escort mission to Saarbrucken, with two wing tanks, when the bumps in the runway bounced him into the air with inadequate air speed. He wobbled and mushed across the treetops and finally crashed down out of sight. His wingtip had hardly disappeared when a huge column of bright flame exploded up. Nobody gave him one chance in a thousand.

1st Lt. Dike R. Pisegna from Group Headquarters hopped fences and ran across fields to the scene and found – two shattered gas tanks and a scorched area by somebody's bean patch, a detached twin row radial engine steaming in someone's back yard, an intact fuselage, nose down on top of a truck with the tail just clearing the side of a house in a small village and Ray himself sitting in the living room of the house across the street. He was badly burned about the face and wrists, and shocked and a month later still in the hospital – but he's still with us. [Andy Wilson of the 507th remembers: 'I was a witness to the crash of Capt. Ray Langford's plane. I was on the south side of the east/west runway. His plane was struggling to pull up heading east. The nose of the plane came up. It sailed nose up without climbing. It hit something (brush?). Wing tanks of gasoline fell off and flamed. It mushed out of sight, nose up, tail down, very scary. And out of sight – until we heard that he had survived and was discovered sitting very shocked, with a shocked lady, in her sitting room, in the first street from the airstrip in Bransgore.']

1st Lieutenant Robert W. 'Bob' Green had his close call on take-off also, banged a wingtip in the tops of some trees, since cut down. And Freddie Fredendall could only say 'I heard the music, that's as close as I want to come' when he returned from a three-hour mission with his tail wheel doors peeled back like the top of a sardine can, and jammed with brush after skimming a three foot hedge at the west side of the field on take-off.

Most anxious men of the month were 1st Lieutenant Duane D. 'Out-Hout' Inthout, sweating out his plane the first time, one of our new pilots flew it on a mission, and Capt. 'Lad' Lutman hounding the S-2 section for his Air Medal. 'It's not that that the Lad is really worried about the medal, he would say, 'hell a little ribbon don't mean a damn to me. But if I get enough of them fast enough I might get back to see the wife and kids by Christmas, see.'

Good natured Lad also rated some sort of recognition as the most browned off man in the squadron on the 11 May escort mission to Saarbrucken, when his flight was fired upon three times by B-24s. 'Hell, he said, 'if those guys shoot at me again I'm going to shoot back. It's them or me. We were going down to protect a straggler and they were just firing all over the place.'

After three missions escorting B-26s, the boys decided that bomber pilots who could fly straight and level though four miles of flak were pretty good after all. Only sour note was the mission of 28 May to Chartres when the B26s flew all round Chartres, which was plainly visible to us, and then bombed somewhere else. The Colonel leading our group finally asked the bombers in exasperation, 'Do you have the slightest idea of where you are and why?'

Most embarrassed man of the month was Major Tice. Visited by a couple of old Fifth Air Force friends in Lockheed P-38 Lightnings, he took a P-38 up for a quick turn around the field and flew with one quarter flaps down to stabilise the aircraft a low speed. In 1942 he ran up 100 combat hours on '38s, covered the battle of the Bismarck Sea, strafed the Kokoda trail and bombed it, and got himself two Zeros. 'It's just been so long since I handled one,' he explained as he fined himself ten dollars, 'but it sure felt good. I still think they handle lighter and better than the '47, for all their weight and extra engine.'

Between missions during the early part of the month, all the pilots banded together into a labour force, policed up two large glider crates and a corrugated iron ammunition shelter and made themselves a comfortable briefing room and snack bar. Major Tice taxied the 'clee track' around for the heavy pushing and hauling, while 1st Lieutenants Sherman N. Crocker, 'OutHout' Int-Hout and 2nd Lieutenant Leroy Graham acted as carpenters in chief. [The Cleveland Cletrac M27 ton high-speed tractor was used by the USAAF for towing aircraft and heavy ground equipment.]

At the end of the month the gang was intact, respectful of flak but confident, still wondering where the hell the Luftwaffe kept itself and ready for invasion. 'I know just where they are going in' said 2nd Lieutenant Floyd F. Blair. 'They are going to land on both sides of the Cherbourg peninsula and cut that thing off. There's all kinds of good beaches around there.'

Historical Report
508th Fighter Bomber Squadron, 404th Fighter Bomber Group,
APO 505, US Army, May 1944
William F Miller, Capt. Air Corps Intelligence Officer, 10 June 1944

1. Organisation:
May 17th 1944, 1st Lt. Raymond F. Gay jr, 2nd Lts. Denzil B. Lee, Charles R. Koerner Elton B. Long, F/O William W. Donohoe joined squadron. [F/O stood for Flight Officer, a rare grade in the USA, lower than 2nd Lieutenant but higher than a non-commissioned officer]
May 18 1944 1st Lt. Felix Markow joined squadron.

2. Strength:
May 31 1944 59 Officers and 254 enlisted men.

3. Date of arrival and departure for stations occupied in the ETO:
Stationed at Station 414 for period May 1 to May 31 1944.

4. Losses in action:
Negative

5. Awards and decorations:
Negative

On May 11 1944, this squadron became operational, fulfilling the hopes and desires of all its members since activation. The first mission was uneventful, but due to the tension of going into combat for the first time it will be remembered by all members of the squadron as one of our most difficult missions.

'Bogies' [unidentified aircraft] were undoubtedly 'Bandits' [enemy aircraft], all flak no matter how inaccurate was 'accurate, heavy, intense' – the highest official categorisation describing flak activity as reported in the mission reports. The briefing was very detailed and lengthy and the interrogation a frenzy of mixed emotions and exuberant tales. Happily enough, when the smoke of battle had cleared we concluded it to be an uneventful fighter sweep. On the same day we had another fighter sweep, this time making a deeper penetration into France and this mission too was uneventful.

Having once broken the ice with our first mission, we were set now to take everything that might come in stride, but in swept bad weather and back again to the tortuous grind of listening to intelligence officers in ground school, a horrible ordeal.

May 7 1944, good weather again favoured us and the squadron had its first dive-bombing mission. Col. McColpin, our Group Commander led the mission as well as our first two, due to the fact that Major Moon, our Squadron Commander, was flying with another group to gain some combat experience. We dive-bombed marshalling yards at Arras with very good results.

May 8 1944 found the boys very excited returning from a fighter sweep. They had seen their first enemy aircraft. ME109s and FW190s were seen between Chalons and Reims but they didn't attack. Major Moon led our squadron for the first time on this mission.

May 9 1944 found our boys attacking a rocket gun target [V1 launch site]. Direct hits were observed on the target, and flak that had everybody holding their breath were encountered at Neufchatel. Again, on the 9th, we flew top cover for the 507th Squadron, which attacked another rocket gun target and this mission was very uneventful. May 10 1944 again we were blasting railroads, attacking the yards at Arras. Major Moon and Bob Johnson cleared the target area of flak by dropping fragmentation bombs on the target before the remainder of the group attacked. They flew so low they had to turn to avoid colliding with the water tower of the town.

May 11 1944 found our boys escorting heavies for the first time. It was a gruelling mission of four hour's duration. Joe Sherwood, our Operations Officer, led this mission and upon returning said his seat was worn out and he wanted to know where the hell the Luftwaffe was. After all, going to Saarbrucken on a long four-hour mission was long enough for Goering to send up some of his boys and if he had to wear out his seat for four hours Herr Goering should send up some planes to relieve the boredom.

May 13th 1944, again we were top cover while the 506th and 507th squadrons of our group dive-bombed the marshalling yard at Tournai. The mission was uneventful.

May 19 1944, ours was Beaumont sur Oise Airdrome but weather made it impossible for us to attack. However, we had our first encounter with Jerry. Six ME109s jumped our squadron near Rouen which was extremely unfortunate for them. When the shooting was over we had our first victory. Ben Kitchens dove after a 109 from 12,000 feet and caught him at 500 feet and shot him down. On take-off Jack Connor failed to get his heavily loaded Thunderbolt in the air and crashed at the end of the runway considerably damaging his aircraft. Everyone heaved a sigh of relief when they saw Jack jump out of his ship uninjured. Jack said that this was the time he heard those bells ringing.

May 20th 1944, again we served as escort for B26s attacking Evreux Fauville airdrome near Paris. Mission was uneventful.

May 21 1944, our mission was to attack rolling stock Southeast of Paris but bad weather forced us to return without making an attack.

May 22 1944 found our boys on what Drexel Morgan called the 'milk run' – as easy as the milkman delivering milk door-to-door. We were ordered to attack Bethune for the third time and our pilots found it great sport to tear up the railway yards again.

May 23 1944, again we served as guardian angels to B26s attacking targets in the Caen area. Mission was uneventful.

May 24th 1944 found us again on what our pilots called the seat hardener mission. On this occasion, we escorted B24s to Paris and returned. Upon interrogation Sam Selkregg shouted with his buoyant enthusiasm 'No Hits, No Runs, No Errors' meaning mission uneventful.

May 25 1944. Our mission was escorting B26s to Liege, Belgium, and again results uneventful.

May 28 1944, again we escorted B26s to Liege. Mission uneventful.

May 29 1944. Our mission was to escort Bl7s returning from Berlin. Our squadron made its deepest penetration into the continent. Making rendezvous with the bombers at Grebenham was uneventful, but bad luck dogged our take-off and landing. Harry Nystrom failed to get his heavily laden ship in the air and crashed on the end of the runway. He luckily escaped without a scratch. Ed Pounds caught some flak in the tail of his ship and his tail wheel failed to lower when he landed. His ship was under control at first but with no tail wheel his ship became unmanageable and rather than crash into some ships that were taxiing, he jammed on the brakes and his ship nosed over and went on its back. Ed escaped with only a small cut on his head, a very lucky pilot.

> *May 30 1944, our mission was to escort heavy bomber stragglers from Holland. Mission uneventful.*
>
> *May 31 1944 found us again to be supporting heavy bombers, but old man weather dogged us and rendezvous was not made. Joe Landa said he heard the bells ringing when he spun from 15,000 feet while in the overcast, finally pulling out at 2,000 feet, a harrowing experience.*
>
> *Summarising May, we find the squadron flew a total of 22 missions with a breakdown as follows; 3 fighter sweeps, 7 dive-bombing missions, and 12 escort missions. After a month of operations every member of the squadron recognised that our excellent record was due to the tireless work and excellent leadership of Major Leo C. Moon.*
>
> *We are happy to report we dropped forty two and a half tons of bombs, successfully escorted B26s, B24s and Bl7s, destroyed one enemy aircraft and suffered no casualties among our ranks.*
>
> *Also, due much credit for the success of our squadron in May are the enlisted men of our squadron whose tireless efforts enabled us to accomplish our excellent record.*

These unit histories have been transcribed unedited from the diaries of Second Lieutenant William P. Corley, Air Corps Historical Officer, courtesy of John Leavesley.

11
THE NEW FOREST AT WAR REVEALED

For the generation that endured the war years on the Home Front between 1939 and 1945, much of what they had grown up with was lost forever. Whilst that loss was more often than not the loss of a family member or friend who perished as a consequence of enemy action at home and abroad, the loss of possessions and property was a further erosion of the human need for wellbeing, belonging and familiarity. The loss of property and change to the built landscape was more acute for town and city dwellers who witnessed the devastation of much that was familiar to them, including schools, factories, churches and libraries. As William Bowen recorded, 'Whole streets became piles of debris and caches of vivid memories.'

National interest in preserving what was left of our wartime heritage gathered momentum in the 1970s, and since then surviving buildings and other constructions from the period have been restored, many remains have been photographed and the details have been catalogued. In addition, many sites have been taken into public ownership so as to preserve both the social and built history. Of particular interest to preservationists are former airfield sites and remaining pillboxes, together with associated emplacements. As part of the New Forest Wartime Memories Project, a major survey revealed a number of previously unmarked and unrecorded sites of wartime occupation. These have now been mapped and recorded, the exercise forming part of a wider fact-finding and information-gathering project which better reveals the wartime role of the New Forest and its people.

Before looking at specifics, we must briefly return to the inter-war years. Much was learnt from the first air raids on Britain during the First World War,

A surviving pillbox located close to the railway at Christchurch. (NFNPA)

and whilst these events were, in context, extreme at the time, they were not in any way an indication or reflection of what was to befall the country just two decades later. By the 1920s, the consensus was that another war seemed remote, and thoughts of prolonged peace ran high. Between 1928 and early 1932, the agreed formula of the Committee of Imperial Defence was: 'It should be assumed for the purpose of framing the estimates of the fighting services that at any given date, there will be no major war for ten years.' Yet it was also in the 1920s that theoretical planning for another 'emergency' was addressed by various government agencies and departments, and consideration was given to, for example, the impact of attacks on the civilian population.

Curiously, some might say, in parallel with this the armed services were being run down. There was no building programme and no plans for wartime infrastructure. In the minds of the public, it was only in the late 1930s that the British government actually woke up and took notice, when the effects of widespread devastation and destabilisation caused by the bombing of Spanish cities during that country's Civil War became known. Across Britain at this time sites including farm outbuildings, empty factories and other premises were surveyed and registered as potential mortuaries, should the need arise. In the

New Forest, many parishes offered their churches for this use. The survey was based on the estimated number of casualties that the country would suffer in the early days of another 'emergency', these estimates arising from think tanks that had met in the previous decade.

Yet there was a contradiction between what the government was doing and what it was perceived to be doing in the face of European and international unrest; between its apparent indifference to war and its intelligence activities, together with the conclusions of various committees. Intelligence-gathering by the government had included enquiring of foreign powers, including Russia, about their experience of war. For example, the Russians were specifically asked about the role of women, as they had been front-line troops for many years. In addition, men returning home to Britain after fighting in the Spanish Civil War were debriefed about their experiences, and much valuable information was gathered.

The RAF Expansion Programme, which began in 1934, evolved from conclusions reached by and discussions during the late 1920s. Sites for new airfields were surveyed and funds were released to construct a total of about ninety new stations, most being on the east coast of England, facing Germany.

Civil Defence and its role in war, to include air raid precautions, was under the care of the Home Office, a decision that was reached by the inter-war committee known as the Committee on the Co-ordination of Departmental Action on the Outbreak of War (CCDAOW).

The changing social and political climates in Europe during the 1930s brought about a marked change in the mood and attitude of some of those in government, as well as in the press and the armed services. It was not a matter of if another war came, but when. In contrast to the belief that mass mortuaries would be needed to accommodate the dead from air attacks, however, Winston Churchill felt that carrying out air raids on Britain would be futile, because air raid shelters would be provided for the entire civilian population.

The Munich Agreement of 1938 bought much-needed time for the country to 'prepare for the inevitable', but by the time war broke out in 1939 small local building contractors who had been given Ministry of Supply work, such as the erection of pillboxes and public shelters, were still recruiting labourers to help meet the need. Larger construction companies had been directed to road building and the construction of airfields, in addition to those already required under the expansion programme. A report dated 3 March 1950 about the financial benefits of the war, and the way ahead for planning and construction, stated: 'Many of today's well known national construction companies including Wimpey and Laing's were contracted to build the major airfields at Beaulieu, Holmsley South, Stoney Cross, Hurn and Christchurch.'

At the peak of the airfield building programme, during the early 1940s, it is estimated that as many as 20,000 workmen were employed across the major sites in the New Forest. The largest airfields swallowed up many acres with vast complexes that included storage sheds and ammunition stores, accommodation blocks and fuel storage, canteens, hangars, boiler houses, control centres, blast shelters, messes for officers and other ranks, and even a gymnasium and a cinema. These were large and densely built conurbations, almost constituting small towns.

Simultaneously across the county, other building projects included the construction of anti-aircraft sites and underground networks, and bunkers to be used as communication and intelligence centres. Nissen huts, inexpensive prefabricated steel structures made from a half-cylindrical skin of corrugated steel, were erected on concrete bases, often in the grounds of requisitioned properties, to be used by Civil Defence, government and armed services agencies. Maycrete buildings were constructed between April and July 1941, although it is incorrect to describe all huts built in a similar temporary style as Maycrete. The total number of Maycrete buildings amounted to just 525, whereas the two main Ministry of Works concrete huts, the Orlit and the BCF, were built in considerably more significant numbers – and their remains can still be found across the country.

Such a demand for construction on an unprecedented scale led to a shortage of manpower and skills. Recruitment of men from Ireland as well as from overseas, including India, Pakistan and Canada, resulted in a substantial increase in the workforce, in the tens of thousands. Temporary 'villages' sprang up across the New Forest to accommodate them. Olive Dickson recorded at the time in her diary that 'Every community throughout our beloved land is touched by the boot of the workman. Be it a small concrete slab for an Observer's Post or a runway stretching out across once green fields, everywhere is a site for war. Concrete that will last for generations, along with the memories and the stories.'

The infrastructure was like a cloth jigsaw, with small and large pieces sewn into a vast picture that was unfolded across the nation. Construction continued apace until 1943, when the last few airfields were completed. Then, on a similar scale, preparations for D-Day began. This included road widening, such as that undertaken at Pilley and on the road between Blackfield and Lepe, the strengthening of bridges, such as those at Beaulieu village and Brockenhurst, the creation of roadside hard standings, slipways, temporary camps including the prisoner-of-war (POW) camps at Setley and additional buildings on existing airfields, including Stoney Cross and Hurn. The Mulberry Harbours were built at sites including Lepe and the Beaulieu River, with up to 10,000 men contributing to the construction and assembly of all the component parts. The entire national infrastructure programme was estimated as costing between £15 billion and £25 billion, with over £4 billion being spent in Hampshire and the New Forest, but in truth the actual sums involved are never likely to be known.

In the immediate aftermath of the war, many buildings were abandoned and others were used for various purposes, including temporary housing for those whose homes had been destroyed in air raids. Requisitioned properties, such as Pylewell House near Lymington and Northerwood House near Lyndhurst, were in most cases returned to their rightful owners. Airfields were stood down and put on a care and maintenance basis, while others, such as Holmsley South, remained in service for a short time until the powers that be decided their fate.

As a child, Alan Tate recalls:

We used to play in the pillboxes and in the control tower near our home in Ringwood. Today I suppose you would liken it to a film set, but to us as eight and nine year olds it was fascinating and fun. Years later, I understood the significance of those buildings and the importance of preserving our history.

That recent history, however, was not something that the vast majority of the population wanted to dwell on, and there was, alongside a need for housing and a return to normal life, a desire to remove and destroy all evidence of war on the Home Front. The government of the day budgeted £65 million to remove as much of the wartime built environment as possible. People wanted to forget about the war and move forward to a brave new world. That brave new world was built using rubble and hardcore from many of the demolished wartime installations, which themselves had originally been built using rubble taken from city streets of blitzed buildings. This was recycling on a vast scale.

Wholesale destruction continued unabated until preservation groups, many born out of post-war social and cultural changes, urged the listing of buildings such as control towers. Interest in the archaeology of the Second World War continues to grow year on year, as does the public's wider interest in Britain's Home Front.

One aspect of archaeological study which has contributed significantly to our understanding of the past is LiDAR. This is a technology used to make high resolution maps, and it has written a new chapter in the recording of newly located sites. In simple terms LiDAR is light and radar: the acronym stands for Light Detection and Ranging. It uses ultraviolet, visible or near infrared light to image objects, and it can be used with a wide range of targets, a narrow laser beam being used to map physical features at a very high resolution. LiDAR was one of the tools at the disposal of the New Forest Remembers project team, which operated under the auspices of the New Forest National Park Authority.

It is worth describing this fascinating process at some length. Initially, wartime diaries were read and assessed by the participating Maritime Archaeology project officer, who recorded references to sites within the study area where a named location or a grid reference was given. Relevant information on the site, for example its type, units in occupation, period of use and a short description, were recorded, as were any other notable events that could be identified. During the Second World War, Britain's armed forces used a mapping system known as the British Modified Military (Cassini) Grid. This meant that the six figure grid references used in the war diaries were totally different to those used by the modern Ordnance Survey, and therefore they needed to be

A laser scanner used to survey the New Forest. (© Forest Research, based on Cambridge University Technical Services)

converted in order to match today's maps. A formula was developed by the Royal Engineers Mapping and Charting Establishment, and the conversion was made with an accuracy of plus or minus 200 metres. It must be remembered that although war diary grid references could be plotted with a reasonable level of accuracy, they were only as accurate as the original reference itself.

In total, 595 locations were identified in the war diaries, and these were researched fully before a comprehensive desk-based assessment (DBA) record was written. Some of these appear below, and they are taken directly from the official record for the sake of accuracy. This information can of course be further researched and cross-referenced via the websites noted below. In addition, many more sites can be located and explored using the relevant references.

Ashley Walk Bombing Range

The government first suggested the compulsory acquisition of land for bombing practice at Ashley Walk, near Godshill in the north of the Forest in November 1939, and the lease was agreed in February 1940. The range was ready to use by August 1940. Ashley Walk bombing range was used by aircraft flying from the Aeroplane & Armament Experimental Establishment (A&AEE) at RAF Boscombe Down. The range consisted of several different targets for bombing, ground attack, mock ship targets, aircraft pens and the Ministry of Home Security target, as well as domestic facilities for crew, two small grass airstrips, observation shelters and towers. The range was used extensively throughout the war, creating many bomb craters and even an aircraft crash site. Activities continued until 1946, but the range was not cleared until 1948. The vast majority of targets and facilities were removed, although the Ministry of Home Security target was covered over with an earth mound instead. Some craters were filled in, but many were left open. Today one observation shelter remains, as do features associated with several others, and chalk markings cut into the ground.

Although the range covered a large area (approximately 5,000 acres) the main targets and construction areas were relatively small-scale structures. Many were temporary in nature, for example the air-to ground targets which were most probably made of scaffolding, and therefore they were unlikely to leave any traces on the ground. Ground markers cut into the ground and lined with chalk were left after the range closed and many are still visible from the air today. However, many of the markers were laid in concrete and although overgrown, are in much better condition. The observation towers and ship target are only indicated by concrete footings that are likely to be very shallow in nature. Owing to the high level of explosives dropped here, there is a possibility of live ordnance surviving in the area.

The only remaining above ground shelter on the range is an observation hut at Ashley Cross. This shelter, built of brick with a concrete roof, is open at the rear and equipped with narrow observation slits facing towards the Fragmentation Target range. When it was built, a bricklayer arranged a 'V for Victory' decoration to be made into the brickwork on all three exterior walls.

Aircraft directional arrow, Ashley Ranges. (Derek Tippets)

Bombing range craters, Ashley Walk. (NFNPA)

SAE Millersford garage and workshop. (Vera Storr)

The surviving viewing post from which observations were made during target practice. (Derek Tippets)

The structure is possibly unique by virtue of being built of brick rather than concrete (generally a preferred material on bombing ranges). However, the brick is imported and not of local type. Conservation work was carried out on the building in 2012.

Millersford
The Armaments Research Department, Millersford, was enclosed in early 1941. The department occupied a near circular area of 650 acres roughly between Deadman Bottom gulley and Millersford Plantation, to the north east of Ashley Range. Between 1941 and its closure in approximately 1949, the centre was engaged in the testing of static bombs and explosives. The site consisted of two main areas, the administrative area being close to the B3080 (to the north of the New Forest) and the explosives testing area to the west. (The B3080 leaves the B3078 at Bramshaw Telegraph at a fork. It heads roughly north-westerly along the county boundary before crossing into Wiltshire just after North Charford. After Redlynch it turns westward and goes through Downton, then crosses the River Avon before Wick, where it ends at traffic lights on the A338.) The administrative area comprised garages, offices and the bomb store and magazine, with the explosives area consisting of a number of pits for detonations, and a number of laboratory buildings, all of which were well protected by turf coverings, and from the latter the explosions could be filmed and assessed.

Brook Common
Searchlight positions were set up across the country throughout the war in order to illuminate enemy aircraft on bombing missions. War diary research has indicated possibly three positions around Brook Common Golf Course. One is listed as in use in 1940, another in 1941 and the third in 1942. It is possible that these all relate to the same site which was used by different units at different times, and its exact grid reference has simply been misreported in the war diaries. Searchlight emplacements came in many different forms during the war. Some were fully mobile, fitted to the back of trucks with an internal generator. Others may have been in sandbagged emplacements, while some

more permanent structures may have had a concrete base and wall along with associated buildings.

Bratley Plain Anti-Glider Obstacles

The NMP (National Mapping Project) has identified this site as a decoy airfield, but the only recorded decoy in this area is at Ridley Plain. It is far more likely that the ditches and banks at this site represent anti-glider obstacles.

In the wake of the fall of France, German invasion became a real threat to Britain. The German deployment of airborne forces had a profound effect on the outcome of fighting on mainland Europe and would certainly have been used in an invasion on the south coast. To prevent gliders from landing, areas of open land such as fields and heathland were covered with materials that would cause a glider to crash. In some instances, poles were erected into the ground, and even obsolete vehicles were used to create obstructions. In some places, banks of earth were erected to make a flat surface more irregular. This was the case at several other locations in the New Forest, including Beaulieu Heath.

Aerial photography indicates that these anti-glider defences were made up of long ditches with mounds of earth piled alongside them, and whilst they are still visible as crop marks from the air today, they appear to have been levelled. The NRHE [National Record of the Historic Environment; searchable at http://www.pastscape.org.uk/] only lists one other example of anti-landing obstacles in England, although it is possible that others do survive nationwide.

Anti-tank islands were defensive points, usually centred on major road junctions, bridges or natural features that when obstructed, would delay the advance of German forces, giving time for Allied reinforcements to move to the area. These sites were usually made up of bunkers, roadblocks, trenches, and in the event of a withdrawal being necessary, explosives that could be used to demolish a bridge or road altogether. War diary research indicates that there were seven roadblocks in and around Lyndhurst and Emery Down in 1941. There is also a concrete block in the garden of Clarendon Villa on Gosport Lane, Lyndhurst that may be relevant to those structures. Road blocks came in various types during the war, including temporary wood and barbed wire obstacles that would not necessarily leave any trace. On the other hand, more complex structures would have involved modifications to the road or the installation of concrete blocks on the verge. It is possible that the structure in Clarendon Villa is an example of this, however, no evidence for bunkers or pillboxes in the Lyndhurst area has come to light. Again, any such installations may have been of a temporary nature and not left any physical trace.

Two searchlight positions at Black Heath are recorded in the war diary research with one known to be in use in 1941 as part of the Southern Indicator & Belts group [this refers to the identification and shooting down of enemy aircraft], and another was in use in 1942. Although the war diaries give slightly different positions for these two, it seems that in all likelihood they were on the same site, and the exact position has simply been misreported in the war diaries. This is supported by the LiDAR survey, which only identifies one potential site on Black Heath. The LiDAR also suggests a large scar that may be trenching and several other pits that may be related.

The LiDAR survey indicates that this is most likely to be a sandbagged or concrete emplacement. Such sites could potentially have left remains below the ground after being removed. Other permanent installations such as cabling for the generator may also be present. Clustered around the site are numerous depressions that may be bomb craters, indicating that the searchlight came under attack from enemy bombers on at least one occasion. The National Mapping Project data lists twenty-two individual records that make up as many as twenty-seven depressions on Black Heath. It is quite possible that these are bomb craters caused by enemy action against the searchlight emplacement. Survey may be able to determine if these are in fact bomb craters or quarrying associated with the searchlight, and further analysis of war diary records may be able to pinpoint an exact date of an attack. However, closer investigation of likely points of defence on the roads into Lyndhurst and in the area around the gun pits may reveal traces of weapons pits and trenches.

Aerial photography indicates that there was a camp at Mogshade Hill from 1944. It is known that Canadian forces were encamped in this area prior to D-Day, and LiDAR survey has revealed the likely location of this camp immediately south of the A31. In the same area, war diary research has indicated the presence of a searchlight position, although a searchlight alone could not account for the level of activity indicated by the aerial photography. However, some structures from the LiDAR survey may represent the searchlight. If this were only a temporary staging camp in advance of D-Day, it is likely that most of the accommodation would have been tented. This may mean that there is little in the way of permanent features such as hard standing or services. However, there may be a great deal of evidence of land levelling to create suitable pitches for tents, vehicle routes and a parade area. A searchlight position may leave a more obvious feature, depending on the type of installation. As this was in all probability an accommodation camp, there is a high likelihood of finding artefacts.

LiDAR survey and aerial photography indicate a system of track-ways, trenches and foxholes at Acres Down and Pilmore Gate Heath and what may be a rifle-range nearby. These are likely to be of Second World War origin although the rifle range may be one of a number built around Lyndhurst in the latter part of the 19th century. Trenches and foxholes in this area would probably have been dug for training purposes as there is no defensive quality to the heath. A large number of nearby shell holes may indicate that live firing was conducted in the area and this is supported by the 1943 New Forest Training Map, which indicates that the area was one of the mortar, grenade and small arms ranges.

The NRHE records 964 examples of Second World War slit trenches of all types, many of which have in fact been removed. The vast majority of these were for genuine defensive purposes at anti-tank islands and airfields or along the coast for example, but practice trenches are rarer. Training trench systems from the First World War are known to survive in Wales, Staffordshire, Northumberland and on Salisbury Plain in Wiltshire. Research and fieldwork at the practice trenches on Salisbury Plain has revealed a great deal of material and personal effects, however, Second World War trenches were not as extensive and were usually a series of unconnected slit trenches and foxholes.

The NMP identifies what might be an Anti-Aircraft (AA or Ack-Ack) battery at Mogshade Hill, based on period aerial photography. Ack-Ack batteries were first established around the New Forest in 1939 and their number grew during the build-up towards D-Day and during deception operations. AA batteries were either heavy, usually housing four or more 3.7 inch guns, or light, using various numbers of 40mm Bofors guns. With one of the most rapid rates of fire, this versatile light anti-aircraft gun was used on both land and sea for over thirty years and was particularly effective against low flying attack aircraft.

The site at Mogshade is visible on 1946 aerial photography as four equally spaced potential gun positions to the south of Mogshade Hill Camp. As such it may have been built to support this camp. However, no reference has been found to this AA position in extensive war diary research or in existing databases. AA batteries were usually quite extensive sites that included services, magazines and accommodation. No such structures are visible near these gun pits, indicating that if it were an AA position, it may have been a very temporary deployment. It may be that any AA guns based here where a support unit of the unit based at Mogshade Camp. Further survey work may be able to reveal the true nature of these features and locate any other features that may be associated with them.

Ridley Plain Bombing Decoy

Bombing Decoy number Q160A was a Q type decoy site which was specifically designed to represent an airfield at night. It was built to direct enemy attention away from Hurn and Holmsley South Airfields. It would have consisted of lighting poles arranged in a pattern similar to an airfield's landing lights, powered by a generator in a small command bunker. The site, and its twin site Q160B at Verwood, were listed as being active in the summer of 1942 only, however the NMP identifies what might be an AA battery at Wilverley Post, based on 1946 aerial photography.

The site at Wilverley is visible on 1946 aerial photography as several potential gun positions alongside the present A35. However, no reference to this AA position has been found in extensive war diary research or existing databases.

Aerial photography has shown a large number of features, including trenches, foxholes and possibly structures at Goatspen Plain. War diary research also indicates the presence of a searchlight emplacement (1942) (WO 166/6099) and a Home Guard observation post (1941) (WO 166/1319) in this location. A circular feature at the north-west end of the identified area may be a searchlight emplacement. Training areas that allowed men to practise trench construction techniques were commonplace during the war. There is however, no record of a live firing range at Goatspen Plain on the 1943 Training Areas map.

Although not a front-line location, further work may reveal information about men and units that trained here before being deployed. Field survey may be able to identify the searchlight emplacement and Home Guard observation post. Recent site visits have noted that the layout of some features may be representative of an organised position rather than foxholes; this may represent the observation post. Aerial photography has shown a large number of features, including trenches, foxholes and possibly structures at Goatspen Plain. War diary research also indicates the presence of a searchlight emplacement and a Home Guard observation post in this location. A circular feature at the north-west end of the identified area may be a searchlight emplacement.

Training areas that allowed men to practise trench construction techniques were commonplace during the war. There is, however, no record of live firing range at Goatspen Plain on the 1943 Training Areas map.

Holmsley South Airfield
RAF Holmsley South was built over the winter of 1941 and 1942 to provide accommodation for units required for Operation Torch in North Africa. It was completed in 1942 as a Class A (permanent) airfield and first used by RAF Coastal Command. Both USAAF and RAF bombers flew patrols form the airfield in 1942 and 1943, before the station was passed to Fighter Command in the build-up to D-Day. The airfield was handed over to the USAAF in July and used by units of IX Bomber Command until October when it was returned to the RAF. It was subsequently used by RAF Transport Command. Regular repatriation flights were flown from the airfield and in September of 1945 and 1946 the airfield hosted public Battle of Britain Day shows. In October 1946, it was reduced to caretaker status (care and maintenance) and later returned to the New Forest.

Despite the fact that the construction of Class A (permanent) airfields represents one of the largest wartime building programmes of the twentieth century in the United Kingdom, relatively few airfields remain in their original condition or a state of good preservation. Like Stoney Cross and Beaulieu, Holmsley South has been levelled and remodelled, although like Stoney Cross, Holmsley's dispersal bays are utilised in a Forest Holidays campsite. These appear to be original concrete in some cases and relaid tarmac in others.

The nature of the construction of the airfield and its ancillary buildings means that there is usually very little potential for below ground features to be identified. Most of the buildings and features had only surface level foundations and today leave little more than concrete bases. Possible exceptions to this rule include the bomb storage area (described below).

Evidence from Beaulieu airfield also indicates numerous below ground communication and services cables and hatches, which may also be present at Holmsley. In the northern area of the airfield (around Stony Moors woodland) is the bomb storage area of the airfield. The access road to the various stores areas is still evident, and several features have been identified in LiDAR survey that correspond with the various stores and preparation areas. Further investigation of this specific area may identify elements of the various sites established here and the extent of any remains. The NRHE only records ninety-nine known bomb stores in the country, and many of these are not actually associated with airfields.

Like Beaulieu and Stoney Cross airfields, the runways at Holmsley were laid in concrete. When the airfields were returned to the New Forest, the concrete was lifted and removed, but at Holmsley, two significant sections remain at the western end, just outside the Crown Lands, along with original perimeter track. Further investigation may reveal in which such runways were laid.

Like most major airbases, Holmsley was equipped with a Battle Headquarters that could serve as a point to co-ordinate defence in the event that the airfield was overrun by ground forces. The Battle Headquarters at Holmsley South, located just off the northern tip of the north–south runway, has been largely (but not completely) blocked up with concrete and the cupola has been removed, but the bunker itself appears to remain below ground.

Rhinefield Training Area
The roughly triangular area of plain that is bordered on the west by the A35, to

the north by Rhinefield Road and the south by Wilverley Inclosure and Burley Road, was recorded as a large Field Firing Area on the 1943 New Forest Training Area Map. War diary research, 33 Army Tank Brigade, has indicated that both infantry and armoured units trained here during the war, and photographs of tank manoeuvres at this location have also been identified in the Imperial War Museum catalogue and in the archives of The Tank Museum at Bovington, Dorset.

The training area has several areas of activity identified in the National Mapping Project data. Additionally, aerial photography has identified further areas of what appear to be shell holes and trenches. Further investigation of these various areas may reveal further detail about the nature of training that took place here. The Training map shows a rifle range immediately east of the Field Firing Area. Additionally, a rifle butt and several chalk markings are clearly apparent on historic aerial photography and as still-visible features on modern aerial photographs. Rifle ranges tended to have a distinct layout. Further investigation of this site may reveal the survival of the features themselves, how typical its layout was and further evidence of the activities that took place here. The area of land north of Wilverley Inclosure shows evidence of numerous shell holes or foxholes and what might be trenches. However, given the use of tanks on these ranges, it is possible that some of the shell holes are in fact gun pits.

Wootton Bridge Depot
Aerial photography indicates what may be a military depot or camp immediately north of Wootton Bridge. Given the proximity of a practice range at Wilverley, it seems possible that this was a depot for stores or ammunition for use in training exercises.

As with many other depots and camps in the New Forest, it is likely that any structural remains will consist of building bases. Modern aerial photography does indicate what appears to be a concrete feature in the centre of the area. It is possible that this is also related. Further investigation may reveal the exact extent of buildings and structures in this area and whether the track on the west side is part of the site or another, unrelated, feature.

Hag Hill Anti-Aircraft Battery

NMP aerial photography indicates what might be an AA battery at Hag Hill, alongside Burley Road.

The site is visible on the 1946 Aerial Photography as are several potential gun positions alongside the road. No reference to this AA position has been found in extensive war diary research, although there is a reference to a searchlight position in the immediate area and on the Home Guard maps of Major Crofton. The battery is also referred to by Desmond Hollier, a boy who lived in Sway during the Second World War, who remembers that 'We had three Anti-Aircraft guns at the top of our road close by the tumulus near to Marlpit Oak, and another three in an old gravel pit on Hag Hill near to Wooton bridge.'

AA batteries were usually quite extensive sites that included services, magazines and accommodation. No such structures are visible near these gun pits, indicating that if it were an AA position, it may have been a very temporary deployment or a Light AA position. Further survey work may be able to reveal the true nature of these features and locate any other features that may be associated with them.

Marlpit Oak Anti-Aircraft Battery

NMP aerial photography indicates what might be an AA battery alongside the Bowl Barrow 800 metres west of Marlpit Oak crossroads. The site is visible on 1946 Aerial Photography records as are several potential gun positions alongside the barrow. AA batteries were usually quite extensive sites that included services, magazines and accommodation. No such structures are visible near these gun pits, indicating that if it were an AA position, it may have been a very temporary deployment or a LAA (Light Anti-Aircraft) position.

Setley Plain Prisoner of War Camp

POW camps across the country could be incredibly varied. Some were requisitioned buildings, while others operated more as hostels for POWs who were believed to be unlikely to attempt escape: these were most notably Italians. However, the Setley site, which stands alongside the A337, is described as a standard-style camp, one of a number nationwide, built to house Italian

Left: Betty Hockey of the Non-Stops in one of the outfits she wore for concerts at Sopley Camp. (Betty Hockey)

Right: Prisoners were happy to help with moving props for the concerts. (Betty Hockey)

```
        Telephone:              MINISTRY OF SUPPLY,
        Bristol 24171
    Please reply to Secretary   HOME TIMBER PRODUCTION
        and quote :             DEPARTMENT,
    Legal WHC/WB                2/7, ELMDALE ROAD,
                                BRISTOL, 8.
    Your Ref.................

    Dear Sir,
                            17th August 1942.

            Prisoners of War Camp - Setley

            Thank you for your letter of the 6th
    instant and I enclose plan for attachment to your
    copy Agreement.

            I enclose cheque for £5/5/0 in payment of
    your charges.

            Payment of the amount due under the Agreement
    will follow in due course from the Chief Account-
    ant.

                        Yours faithfully,

                            (Solicitor)
                        Legal Assistant to the
                            Department.

    Montague Chandler Esq.
    Clerk to the Verderers,
    Abbey Water,
    Romsey,
    Hants.
```

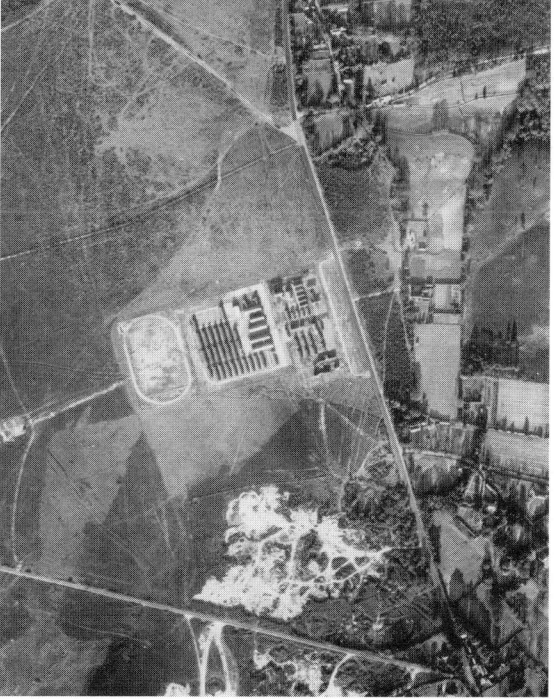

Setley was Prisoner of War Camp 65. (NFNPA)

Opposite bottom left: A document relating to the Setley Camp site. (Author's collection)

Bottom right: An aerial view of Setley Camp, 1946. (NFNPA)

prisoners captured in the North African campaign. It was probably constructed in late 1942 or 1943. Many camps were built by the POWs themselves, to a standard arrangement complete with accommodation huts, garden, canteen, sewage facilities, water tower and accommodation and offices for the Allied troops garrisoning the site. The Italian prisoners at Setley worked on surrounding farms and sawmills. The camp later housed German prisoners, and although some were allowed to leave the camp, this was less prevalent than with the Italians. There is anecdotal evidence of a hut being set alight by some of the POWs, although this needs further investigation. Exactly when Setley was closed is not known from the current records, but it is believed to have still housed men in 1947 and it most likely closed when all POW camps in Britain finally closed in July 1948.

The camp was used to provide housing for gypsy families after the war, possibly until the 1960s. There is no record of its demolition, but modern aerial photography indicates that it has been totally cleared, leaving only building bases and the pattern of the camp. Setley is the only recorded 'standard' camp in the study area. The trace of the site is readily identifiable in aerial photography, suggesting that many ground features still survive.

Brockenhurst Anti-Tank Island
Brockenhurst is not referred to as an anti-tank island in any war diary entries, but is referred to in the papers of Major Crofton who was a Home Guard officer during the Second World War. A map included with these papers identifies an anti-tank ditch at Latchmoor and another at the A337 bridge over the Lymington River. Various other positions are marked, but un-labelled. It has not been established if the areas marked on the Major Crofton map indicate if these defences were ever created or were just particular places, for example, houses to be used to defend in the event of an invasion.

Careys Manor
Careys Manor, Brockenhurst, was built in 1888 as a replacement for a much older hunting lodge that existed in the same area. It is possible that the house hosted a unit of Welsh Guards at some point during the war, but its main role was as the Royal Navy Eastern Warfare School (RNEWS). Exactly when it was requisitioned by the Royal Navy and when it was returned to its owners, and indeed whether it was used to train Royal Navy personnel, Royal Marines or possibly men of SOE Force 136 is not clear from the material so far assessed. As with many other requisitioned houses, ancillary buildings may have been built in the grounds.

Balmer Lawn Hotel
During the Second World War, Balmer Lawn Hotel, on the outskirts of Brockenhurst, was used as a headquarters for various units based in the area. War diary research indicates that it was initially used as HQ for a Royal Marine Division (this may have been the artillery brigade of the Division) and was later occupied by the HQ of the 3rd Canadian Division. In Holland's Wood, which is immediately north of the hotel, there are several features that may be ancillary parts of the HQ.

Large buildings and hotels were frequently requisitioned as HQs for units during the war because they offered space and accommodation for senior officers and for various planning and administrative units, although quite often major changes would be made to interiors to provide appropriate space.

Balmer Lawn Depot

Aerial photography indicates what may be a military depot or camp at Standing Hat near Brockenhurst, which may have been used for the storage of ammunition or supplies. As with many other depots and camps in the New Forest, it is likely that any structural remains will probably consist only of building bases, and as here, modern aerial photography does in fact show what appears to be a concrete feature in the centre of the area.

This archaeology, of course, is not just about the constructed environment and the remains of that environment. It is also about the social impact of the people who came together from all parts of the country and from overseas to share in the common goal of victory and freedom. In doing so, many of them diarised their experiences, shared their stories of home and family, and for a time, they became part of the community and the fabric of wartime life in the Forest.

The road under this bridge at Balmer Lawn was lowered to accommodate the passage of large military vehicles. This was part of the road upgrade programme across the New Forest in 1944. (Author's collection)

It is about the change of a way of life and the demands made upon everyone, and it is about determination, dedication and sacrifice. As we rapidly approach the end of an era that will no longer be within living memory, it is vital that we recognise the value of our archaeology, preserving what can be preserved and memorialising that which cannot.

What makes us the generation we are today stems from the resourcefulness of the previous generation that demonstrated, against great challenges, the capability to build and create on an unprecedented scale, unimaginable today, even with all the technology at our fingertips. The legacy of that era lives on in part through the archaeology of bricks and mortar, galvanised steel and concrete. Our history lies there too.

For further reference about this project and information about sites, please see www.newforestnpa.gov.uk/wwii and http://www.lidar-uk.com/. Please check that the sites you wish to explore are accessible and safe, and above all that access is permitted. It is advisable that information is sought from the relevant agencies, authorities and private landowners before embarking on exploration. A recommended starting point for information is the New Forest Centre, www.newforestcentre.org.uk.

Special thanks and acknowledgements are given to Archaeological Desk Based Assessment, New Forest Remembers, Untold Stories of World War II, Final Report, April 2013. Copyright Maritime Archaeology Ltd, Room W1/95, National Oceanographic Centre, Empress Docks, Southampton, Hampshire, SO14 3ZH.

12
To Conserve and Enhance

Far too often, the country's built wartime heritage is eroded by new developments, be they housing estates, business parks or shopping centres. Another control tower topples, another piece of runway is torn up, a bulldozer crushes another Nissen hut.

Some years ago, I was witness to a conversation between an amateur historian and a landowner after the latter had dismantled a 1942-dated control tower that was an excellent example of its type. After an hour or so, the landowner acknowledged that perhaps he had been too quick off the mark by considering immediate financial gain rather than giving consideration to the long-term benefit of preserving a rare piece of the nation's heritage. Sadly, when it was too late he came up with an idea that would not only have saved the building from demolition, but would also have generated revenue, and in turn would have created a history experience for visitors.

This perhaps highlights a lack of policy when and where it is needed to safeguard not only buildings, but also the memory of all those who served. Immediately after the Second World War, there was a concerted effort to dismantle as much as possible of the infrastructure of the wartime Home Front. Whilst it was practical, for example, to sell off trucks to commercial enterprises to help bump-start the post war economy, and whilst many 'bombed out' civilians took up temporary residence in former POW camps and barrack blocks, a huge demolition programme saw a speedy end to entire installations, many of which had only been built three to four years previously.

Little can be seen of the Advanced Landing Grounds at Winkton and Bisterne, but deep underground, on part of the former Winkton site, is a relic

A surviving building on the site of the former airfield at Winkton. (Author's collection)

Below: Site of the former Cold War bunker close to the former airfield at Winkton (Author's collection)

Freda Belle II was one of the many aircraft flown from Winkton. (John Leavesley)

of the Cold War. A regional seat of government, housed within a huge three-storey bunker, it is now being used for document storage. It is on private land.

The public and the government had had enough of war and they wanted to look forward, not dwell on the recent past. Moreover, the nation's mindset after years of hardship, rationing and austerity was still to make the best use of what it had through recycling; the example has already been given of the demolished buildings that were used as hardcore for new roads. The programme to rebuild Britain inevitably led to the wholesale destruction of sites that today we would recognise as being of significant historical value. Thankfully, not all was lost: a number of airfields were given over to civilian use and others became industrial parks. (I mention airfields in particular because of all the wartime developments these sites were the largest, with the greatest impact on the area and within the community in which they were constructed.) Right across the country it is still

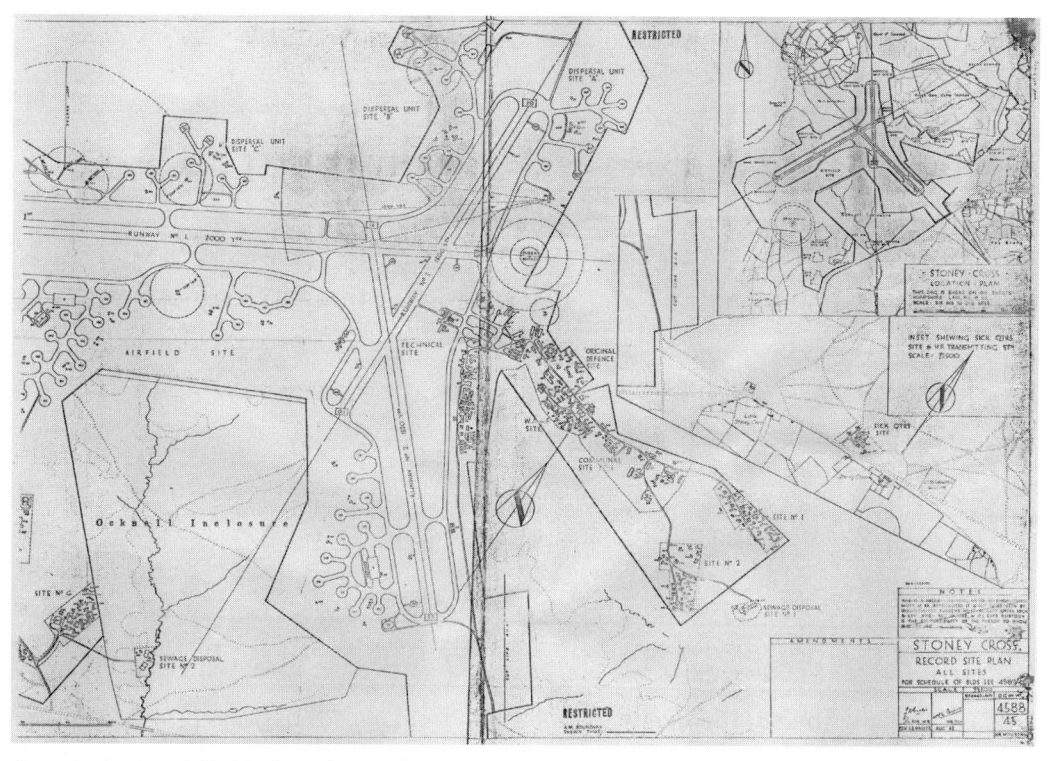

Stoney Cross airfield plan. (NARA)

possible to stumble upon evidence of wartime activity. By way of an example, only recently I was shown a long length of cabling in a tree, which had been there since 1944 when the telephone lines were cut and the poles were taken away from what was a USAAF ALG airfield, near Lymington. A few miles away, and a few inches below the soil near a farmhouse, it was possible to locate more cabling; and nearby was a junction box hanging off a wall. A step further across the Forest, and a single brick building was just visible through some dense foliage. I was told it had been a latrine! The site returned to farmland after the war, and the copse that had been chopped down to make way for some blister hangars has been steadily regrowing for the past seventy years.

On the front line of defence in the years leading up to and during the war, the New Forest was to become pivotal in the preparations for, and launch of,

D-Day. Given its geographical location, its varied open and wooded landscape and its proximity to the sea, it is not surprising that as long ago as the sixteenth century the Forest was being used for 'military training that will enhance and harden the fighting skills of the men in conflict at home and abroad'. It was here for example, that the South Hants Militia, operating from Exbury, was training to defend the south coast against a possible invasion by the Spaniards who, it was thought, would land on the Isle of Wight. Over the subsequent centuries the South Hants Militia, eventually became part of the Hampshire Regiment, then after the Second World War the Royal Hampshire Regiment. The 1st Battalion of the Regiment formed part of the 50th (Northumbrian) Infantry Division, and took part in the D-Day landings on Gold Beach on 6 June 1944.

Surveyed by the War Department in the mid-1930s as an area that would be ideal for a multitude of uses associated with military activity, the Forest gave continual service for many centuries for the training of soldiers. During the First World War it was a vast holding camp for Allied soldiers heading for the trenches, yet in another emergency the Forest would be used even more extensively to serve the needs of the RAF, the navy and the army as well as serving thousands of Allied service personnel.

In addition to tank driver training, small arms training, bomb ranges, SOE 'houses', a vast tented city for over 100,000 troops with capacity to expand, the building of Motor Torpedo Boats (MTBs), the creation of Stop Lines, a large Secret Army and everything else that comes as part of the package of war preparation and defence, the Forest had twelve airfields operational at the time of 6 June 1944. Only Hurn Airfield, now Bournemouth International Airport, survives, although the former RAF Calshot, without most of the obvious signs of wartime occupation, operates as an activities centre.

The New Forest National Park was created in March 2005 and the New Forest National Park Authority took up its full powers in April 2006. It is now working in partnership with other New Forest organisations to help achieve its two statutory purposes; to conserve and enhance the natural beauty, wildlife and cultural heritage of the Park, and to promote opportunities for the understanding and enjoyment of its special qualities.

Whilst much of the landscape we see today has been shaped by man over many thousands of years, the impact of the Second World War has strongly influenced much of the National Park's character, architecture and landscape. The surviving visible structures of air-raid shelters, installations, former airfields and bombing ranges all play their role. For the full impact of this evidence on the landscape, it is often best viewed from the air. But now that much of the landscape has been restored to its pre-war use, landmarks such as the former RAF airfield at Ibsley have been lost, although some buildings such as the control tower still remain.

Wartime buildings were once commonplace, but they are now increasingly regarded as rare survivors of a tumultuous period in our history. Because of their important role, they are now being considered for Listed Building status or Scheduled Monument Statutory Protection, and with this in mind the New Forest National Park Authority is working hard to retain a number of wartime structures by negotiating with land managers and creating Landscape Management Agreements.

The Authority has made it a requirement for detailed records to be created when it is not viable or practical to retain wartime structures. By keeping a record such as drawings and photographs, future generations will be able to appreciate the buildings and structures and the vital contribution they made to our heritage. Although a number of temporary wartime military buildings often found new uses after the war and others were moved to new sites or converted for domestic use, new planning requirements include the need for detailed records for any such building that the owners have been given permission to demolish.

Frank Green of the Park Authority says that his organisation is working hard to update public records of Second World War structures and air-raid shelters that have not previously been recorded, through a series of archaeological field surveys and routine site visits:

> As part of a major national project, a detailed archaeological survey is being carried out on the New Forest coastline and maritime environment. This work will increase our knowledge of the Park's maritime sites in Lymington and Southampton Water. For example, work has previously

TO CONSERVE AND ENHANCE

Spitfires from Ibsley flew in support of the D-Day landings. (Author's collection)

A well-preserved air raid shelter at Ashurst near Totton. (Author's collection)

167

located uncatalogued Luftwaffe aerial photographs taken for the German U-boat division of the Kriegsmarine. Research of the national archives indicates that there is a vast number of documents available for research. Top secret documents about Operation Overlord and D-Day are now publicly available and this material offers a greater insight into the role that the Forest played during the war. The Second World War will always be subject to public interest and research, and it is imperative that we continue to investigate and record how people managed their lives during the war period.

Whilst it is known that the larger country houses were used by the military as operational bases and as hospitals and for institutional purposes, many smaller houses were requisitioned to store important collections from national museums. Many social details about the New Forest during wartime are still cloudy; for example, there is now an initiative to discover how a large party of Irishmen who were building the Mulberry Harbours on the Cadland Estate were housed and fed. Details of this party and similar groups are poorly recorded, and often the only way to find out is to talk to those who were there at the time.

It is vital to continue to promote and encourage local oral history projects to fill in the blanks, not only to understand local traditions, but also to gain personal stories of people's memories about the war years: memories of how people coped with rationing, of bombing and air-raids, what they did in their spare time, or quite simply how the war changed their lives. This will help to build up the type of account that we can all understand the humorous events and the everyday activities of adults and children living and surviving in this tough period of history. We should not forget that the war brought together many people with others from very different social backgrounds, possibly through their work or by being billeted or lodging as an evacuee. City children often experienced their first taste of the countryside and the freedom and adventure that the Forest afforded them, as well as the experience of developing lifelong friendships and surrogate families. Frank Green again: 'We should be collecting as many memories as we can of how the war affected those who were living and working in the New Forest and how it changed the lives of our parents and grandparents while they are still with us.' The National Park Authority is just one organisation that is working hard to bring groups and individuals together to protect their wartime legacy because of its educational and historical value.

The last words should be given to John Whitmore, writing in 1943:

The Forest is the greatest of all ironies, the gentle running streams, the majestic trees, the breathtaking views, the animals that roam as free as they wish, while men who come here in time of war have no freedom, no majesty, no gentleness, for we are engaged in the destruction of Forest lands with our tanks, our airfields, our camps and our heavy boots upon the rich earth.

And it is in the rich soil of our country that we lay our dead who from this Forest set out to win freedom, their lives then shortened by the bullet and the bomb. Yet in years to come the trees will still grow, the streams will still flow while our history fades beneath the feet of future generations who may ask, what happened here in this place of such enduring beauty.

Postscript

In August 1939, Alan Brooke was appointed head of Southern Command, and on the outbreak of the Second World War he went to France as a member of the British Expeditionary Force. Brooke returned to Britain, and in July 1940 he replaced Edmund Ironside as commander of the Home Forces. In this post, Brooke had several major disagreements with Winston Churchill about military strategy, so it came as a surprise when in 1941 Churchill appointed him Chief of Imperial Staff. He was to become Churchill's most important military adviser, and he was promised command of Operation Overlord in 1944 – although the role was given to General Eisenhower at the insistence of President Roosevelt.

Brooke's diaries make fascinating reading, especially as he later added to the original notes that he made during the war.

> *I considered the invasion a very real and probable threat and one for which the land forces at my disposal fell far short of what I felt was required to provide any degree of real confidence in our power to defend these shores. It should not be construed that I considered our position a helpless one in the case of an invasion. Far from it! We should certainly have a desperate struggle and the future might well have hung in the balance, but I certainly felt that given a fair share of the fortunes of war we should certainly succeed in finally defending these shores. It must be remembered that if my diary occasionally gave vent to some of the doubts which the heavy responsibility generated, this diary was the one and only outlet for such doubts.*

The question of whether the defences that were created would have been effective in invasion is vexed. In mid-1940, preparations relied heavily upon field fortifications. The First World War had made it clear that assaulting prepared defences with infantry was deadly and difficult, but similar defences in Belgium had been overrun by well-equipped German Panzer (tank) divisions in the early weeks of 1940, and with so many armaments left at Dunkirk, British forces were woefully ill equipped to take on German armour. On the other hand, while British preparations for defence were ad hoc, so were the German invasion plans. A fleet of 2,000 converted barges and other vessels had been hurriedly made available but their fitness for purpose was debatable; in any case, the Germans could not land troops with all their heavy equipment. Until the Germans captured a port, both armies would have been short of tanks and heavy guns.

The later experiences of the Canadian Army during the disastrous Dieppe Raid of 1942, American forces on Omaha Beach on D-Day and when Japanese defenders on Pacific Islands were taken on showed that under the right conditions a defender could exact a terrible price from assaulting forces, significantly depleting and delaying enemy forces until reinforcements could be deployed appropriately.

In the event of invasion, the Royal Navy would have sailed to the landing places, possibly taking several days. It is now known that the Germans planned to land on the southern coast of England. One reason for this was that the narrow seas of the English Channel could be blocked with mines, submarines and torpedo boats. While German naval forces and the Luftwaffe could have extracted a high price from the Royal Navy, they could not have hoped to prevent interference with any attempt to land a second wave of troops and supplies that would have been essential to German success, even if by then the Germans had captured a port and were able to bring in significant heavy equipment. In this scenario, British land forces would have faced the Germans on more equal terms than otherwise, and it would only have been necessary to delay the German advance, preventing collapse until the German land forces were, at least temporarily, isolated by the Royal Navy and then mounting a counter-attack. Scholarly consideration of the likely outcome of invasion,

POSTSCRIPT

including that of the 1974 Royal Military Academy, indicates that while German forces would have been able to land and gain a significant beachhead, Royal Navy intervention would have been decisive, and even with the most optimistic assumptions the German army would not have penetrated further than GHQ Line and therefore would have been defeated. Following the failure to gain even local air superiority in the Battle of Britain, Operation Sea Lion was postponed indefinitely: Hitler and his generals were aware of the problems of an invasion. Hitler was not ideologically committed to a long war with Britain, and many commentators suggest that German invasion plans were a feint never intended to be put into action.

While Britain may have been militarily secure in 1940, both sides were aware of the possibility of political collapse. If the Germans had won the Battle of Britain, the Luftwaffe would have been able to strike anywhere in southern England, and with the prospect of an invasion the British government would have come under pressure to agree terms. However, the extensive anti-invasion preparations demonstrated to all that whatever happened in the air the United Kingdom was able and willing to defend itself.

The New Forest, on the south coast of England and therefore within range of enemy air power and vulnerable to attack from the sea, had by 1944 become one of the cornerstones of the nation's ability to strike back. As the historian Alan Morris reminds us:

> *The stretch of private beach at Needs Oar is littered with brick work and concrete from the various emplacements and the myriad of smaller constructions which once dominated the shoreline. Debris from the heavily camouflaged AA gun sites can also be found. From the air, as with most of the Forest airfields and installations, imprints left as a result of previous usage, can be clearly seen.*

The Forest continues to fascinate historians, researchers, writers and artists. The Second World War has left a considerable legacy, which manifests itself in many different ways – including those of a less tangible nature. One veteran wrote a poem after his return to the area in 1962:

This cottage is one of many properties across the New Forest which are said to be haunted by the ghosts of airmen. (Author's collection)

One of the tangible legacies of war. These servicemen are laid to rest in Bransgore. (Maxine Knott)

POSTSCRIPT

The ghosts of yesterday roam freely across the forest floor
You hear them when they walk up the steps and open the barrack door
Hello, who's there, you cry in a startled voice
There is never an answer, just an eerie noise.

And when you stand on that deserted, broken runway
You will hear a ghost plane fly by, another sortie, another day
You look skywards there is nothing there, just a vast empty space
But you are convinced you glimpsed the young pilot's face.

In the distance a telephone rings in a deserted mess room
You run towards the sound, breathless, get there soon
But as suddenly as the ringing of the phone bell reached your ears
It was gone, was it real, your doubts are now mixed with fears.

Then passing by along a tree-lined Forest lane
A man and girl in uniform, to you it seems quite plain
They ride a vintage motorbike, it's painted military green
So you glance again, nothing there, nothing to be seen.

The spirits of men and machines seem as though they want to live on
From a far off age, yet still in living memory for some
So many people have experienced these spirits and they will say
The spirits will never rest, they will remain with us day upon day.

They want to remind us of the futility of war
To remind us of their own sacrifice which they put to the fore
'We went over to the spirit world, we had no choice
Remember us, we still have a presence even though we have no voice.'

Deep in the Forest are obvious signs of military occupation. (NFNPA)

References

Some references are given for information only. Access to some sites may be restricted or prohibited. If you intend to visit individual sites, do please check in advance whether the land is private, restricted or in public use. We do not recommend you attempt to access land and property without the relevant permissions that may be required. Please be aware that where public access is usually permitted, from time to time activities including timber felling, scheduled farm work and ground nesting may mean access is temporarily suspended or restricted. Furthermore, please note that the Forest is used extensively by horse riders, and every care must be taken when travelling through the area.

Please also refer to information provided within the book, relevant to other sites and to the appropriate official organisations. When travelling through the area please take into account access during the peak holiday season and please use designated car parks. There are accredited camping sites in the New Forest and designated footpaths and tracks.

Several organised walks across the Forest pass by or through some former wartime sites of interest.

New Forest Walks: A Time Traveller's Guide
Walk One takes in the Ashley Walk Bombing Range near Godshill.
Walk Four features the 'Portuguese Fireplace' and the site of a First World War narrow gauge railway associated with the sawmill near Millyford Bridge.
Walk Eight takes in the Trench Mortar School and War Dog Training area on Matley Heath, near Lyndhurst.

Walk Ten features Beaulieu Heath's Second World War airfield.
Walk Eleven features the wartime use of the Balmer Lawn Hotel at Brockenhurst.
Walk Sixteen features another section of the Ashley Walk Bombing Range.

New Forest Walks, A Seasonal Wildlife Guide
Walks in this guide pass beside or through sites of a nineteenth-century Volunteers Rifle Range near Hampton Ridge, the site of the Armaments Research Department, Millersford, Second World War bomb craters near Pignal Hill, the site of an anti-aircraft battery command post on Yew Tree Heath and a large mound on Beaulieu Heath used as a backstop to targets used during the testing of aircraft machine guns.

New Forest Explorers Guide website
Walks featured here are Brockenhurst's Volunteers Rifle Range, Beaulieu Heath Second World War airfield, the Setley Plain POW camp and White Moor, near Lyndhurst which was a military training and holding area.

Sources of information about land ownership include the Land Registry Service and local Parish, Town and County Councils relevant to the area in which the land lies. Another source is http://en.wikipedia.org/wiki/Operation_Sea_Lion_:_The_Sandhurst_Wargame.

New Forest Remembers project
Hundreds of articles, photos, documents, films and audio recordings relating to the First and Second World Wars.
http://www.newforestheritage.org/

Also useful
http://www.landregistry.gov.uk/
http://www.newforest.gov.uk/
http://www.newforesttrust.org.uk/
http://www.newforestnpa.gov.uk/
http://newforest.gov.uk/index.cfm?articleid=5197

REFERENCES

OTHER SOURCES OF INFORMATION
(This is not intended to be an exhaustive list)

Ringwood Tourist Information Centre
The Furlong
Ringwood
Hampshire, BH24 1AZ
01425 470896

The Verderers of the New Forest
The Queen's House
Lyndhurst
Hampshire, SO43 7NH
023 8028 2052

The New Forest Volunteer Rangers
http://www.newforestvrs.org.uk/forest-history/New Forest Explorers Guide
www.newforestexplorersguide.co.uk

The Real New Forest Guide
http://www.thenewforestguide.co.uk/, especially the page relating to Ashley Walk Bombing range: http://www.newforestvrs.org.uk/forest-history/new-forest-explosives/ashley-walk-bombing-range/

Hampshire Airfields
This site provides a page on each Hampshire airfield, with a brief history.
www.hampshireairfields.co.uk

Friends of the New Forest Airfields
https://fonfasite.wordpress.comRAF Ibsley Historical Group
www.rafibsley.co.uk

RAF Ibsley Airfield Heritage Trust
www.ibsleytower.info

A History of Avon Castle
http://avoncastle.net/html/history.html

National Motor Museum, Beaulieu
SOE exhibition, which is on permanent display.
https://www.beaulieu.co.uk/attractions/secret-army-exhibition/

British Resistance Archive
http://www.coleshillhouse.com/
For Hampshire Auxiliary Unit patrols and Operational Bases see
http://www.coleshillhouse.com/hampshire-auxiliary-units-and-obs.php

The New Forest Airfields Memorial
Black Lane, Holmsley South, Bransgore, Christchurch, Dorset, BH23 8EB
(OS reference SZ 208 987)
http://inewforest.co.uk/places/new-forest-airfields-memorial/

Wessex Film and Sound Archive
Hampshire Record Office
Sussex Street
Winchester
Hampshire, SO23 8TH
01962 846154
www3.hants.gov.uk/wfsa.htm

BBC News: Hampshire & Isle of Wight
'In pictures: Memories of life and work in the New Forest during WW2'
http://www.bbc.co.uk/news/uk-england-hampshire-24806535

REFERENCES

WARTIME SITES

This list is by no means exhaustive, and is only intended to give a snapshot of some of the interesting sites associated with the wartime history of the New Forest.

A visit to the New Forest Centre and Museum at Lyndhurst (follow brown heritage signs) is highly recommended, and Lyndhurst is also a good starting point from which to explore the Forest.

The New Forest Centre
Lyndhurst
Hampshire, SO43 7NY
023 8028 3444
http://www.newforestcentre.org.uk/

The St Barbe Museum and Art Gallery, also in Lymington, is also a good point from which to start a tour. It reopened in July 2017 after a £2 million transformation.

St Barbe Museum and Art Gallery
New Street
Lymington
Hampshire, SO41 9BH
01590 676969
http://www.stbarbe-museum.org.uk/

The sites mentioned below are not accessible to the public unless otherwise stated and explorers are encouraged to establish the status of such sites and private accessibility (if any) with the relevant owners and the authorities. In particular, please note that it is illegal and potentially very dangerous to access pillboxes along railway lines; the photographs included in this book were taken when accompanied by railway staff.

Almost all former Second World War airfields display memorial plaques, many of which were organised under the auspices of New Forest historian the late Alan Brown.

ASHLEY RANGES (B3078)
Also known simply as 'The Ranges', this valley straddles the main road between Fordingbridge and Brook in the north of the Forest, and was used for bomb aiming practice. The famous 'Bouncing Bomb' was trialled here. The area was used for target practice for fighter pilots. A track known as Snake Road leads to the remains of the site, including marker and observation points.

BASHLEY
Ossemsley Manor, just outside the village of Bashley, was no. 624 Camp for German POWs. The exact location of the camp within the grounds has not been identified by English Heritage. After some time in the 1960s and 1970s as a country club, Ossemsley Manor has now been divided into flats.
No access

BEAULIEU (B3504, from Hatchet Pond towards Lymington)
To the left the Isle of Wight is visible, and to your right the land is open and expansive. This is the site of Beaulieu's Second World War airfield: some brick and concrete remains are clearly visible. The site is partially accessible.

THE BEAULIEU ESTATE
This was requisitioned, and became an SOE training centre, or a Finishing School as they were also known. Each section had its own 'house', with French and German agents being sent to those countries after training. There were over fifty SOE training bases across the country, agents being kept separate from each other.

At Hill Top, junction with Exbury Road and B3054, there are some SOE training houses, now in private ownership. Stand at Hill Top with Beaulieu village behind you. The open land to your right was used to create a decoy town to draw enemy aircraft away from Southampton. A few concealed pillboxes were constructed guarding the bridge over the river in Beaulieu village. They were built into existing houses in some cases, and evidence can still be seen. Note the plate on the side of the bridge, which gives the date it was reinforced to cope with heavy military traffic in the build up to D-Day.

REFERENCES

Top left: Parachute silk in one of the SOE display cases. (Beaulieu Estate)

Top right: Secret Army exhibition. (Beaulieu Estate)

Some of the gadgets used by agents. (Beaulieu Estate)

183

BOLDRE (via A337, St John the Baptist's Church)

Visit the memorial to HMS *Hood*. The *Hood*, the largest warship of its time, was sunk on 24 May 1941 with the loss of all but three of the 1,418-strong company, during the Battle of the Denmark Strait. Car parking is available next to the church, which is open to visitors every day from 10am to 4pm.

St John the Baptist's Church
Church Lane
Boldre
Hampshire, SO41 5PG
http://www.bsbb.org.uk/

BRANSGORE (from A35, Lyndhurst Road)

A former Second World War communications bunker was sited here. It was used to direct operations in the Bay of Biscay.

The author meets two members of the Exbury Veterans Association. (Maxine Knott)

For a very short time General George Patton was based at Breamore.

REFERENCES

BREAMORE HOUSE (A338, Breamore village)
After being requisitioned, Breamore House was used by the military during the Second World War, and for two weeks it was General George Patton's HQ. Nearby privately owned Breamore Mill was a fortification on what was known as a Stop Line, which followed the River Avon. There are three pillboxes nearby: see http://www.pillbox-study-group.org.uk/defence-articles/breamore-mill/ for further details, including locations. Breamore House is open to the public for some of the year; the Mill is not.
Breamore House
Nr Fordingbridge
Hampshire, SP6 2DF
01725 512858
breamore@btinternet.com   www.breamorehouse.com

BROCKENHURST
Careys Manor was the Royal Marines Eastern Warfare School. This may have been an SOE training school for jungle warfare. The SOE in the Far East went by the name of Force 136. Today the building is Careys Manor Hotel.

CHRISTCHURCH (A337/B3059 junction in Somerford)
Now a business and industrial park, this was a pre-war airfield with a history that spanned about forty years, from 1926 to the mid-1960s. The buildings have now been demolished.

EAST BOLDRE (B3504 Beaulieu to Lymington road, on the left travelling from Beaulieu) This is the site of a First World War airfield. The village hall is in an original airfield building, which can be viewed from the road.

EXBURY (Exbury House, via B3054)
This is the site of former HMS Mastodon, a centre for naval intelligence and associated activities. It is close to the crash site of the legendary Exbury Junkers in April 1944, and the nearby Beaulieu River was full of craft in the build-up to D-Day. There are memorials in the grounds.

Exbury Gardens and Steam Railway
The Estate Office
Exbury
Southampton
Hampshire, SO45 1AZ
023 8089 1203
https://www.exbury.co.uk

HATCHETT'S POND (B3504, Beaulieu to Lymington road)
The pond was used by the Fire Service, the RAF and the Royal Navy for various water training exercises, and the site is accessible.

HOLMSLEY SOUTH (A35, west of Lyndhurst)
Plenty of airfield concrete hard-standings remain on what is now a major campsite: the former perimeter tracks are used as access roads. Holmsley is also the site of the New Forest Airfields Memorial.

Holmsley Campsite
Forest Road
Christchurch
Dorset, BH23 7EQ
(use BH23 8EB for sat nav)
01425 674502
https://www.campingintheforest.co.uk/england/new-forest/holmsley-campsite

Inside a bomber based at Holmsley South, photographed by a crew member. (Author's collection)

REFERENCES

HORDLE (between New Milton and Lymington, Hampshire)
Walhampton House was an Officers' Rest Centre, a cover name for an Office of Strategic Services (OSS) base. It was officially listed as 'USAAF Station 558. Principal US Units Assigned: Det D, 93 SCSRD; USSTAFE'. It is presently a school. The SOE helped establish and train OSS agents before America's entry into the war, giving that organisation the benefit of its experience.
No access

Walhampton School was used as an OSS station during the Second World War. (Walhampton School)

Aerial view of Walhampton School, 1930. (Walhampton School)

Two youngsters on Walhampton School's front steps, early Second World War. Notice that they have both grown out of their jackets! (Walhampton School)

HURN (B3073, Bournemouth International Airport)
A few scattered Orlit-type buildings survive, including on the perimeter of the airport. It is recommended you contact the airport authorities for further information.
Bournemouth International Airport
Parley Lane
Christchurch Dorset, BH23 6SE
01202 364000 http://www.bournemouthairport.com/

HURST CASTLE (via B3058, Milford on Sea)
Travel by ferry from Keyhaven or on foot from Milford on Sea to this fort, which was originally built by Henry VIII in 1544 as part of a chain of coastal fortresses. The castle was modernised during the Napoleonic Wars and again in the 1870s, when two enormous armoured wings were constructed. During the Second World War, coastal gun batteries and searchlights were installed here. Hurst Castle is managed by Hurst Marine on behalf of English Heritage.
Hurst Castle
http://www.hurstcastle.co.uk/
01590 642344
info@hurstcastle.co.uk
For ferry times see http://www.hurstcastle.co.uk/ferries/

HYTHE (A326)
Motor Launches and MTBs were built here. The former Husbands shipyard has now been demolished. T.E. Lawrence (Lawrence of Arabia) lived here. Hythe is shown in German reconnaissance photographs dating from the early war years.

IBSLEY (via A338)
Remains of a control tower (on private land) can be seen from the road, as can several other buildings as you drive through the area. There is a stone memorial in Ellingham Drove, and also visible are the remains of the end of the main runway.

REFERENCES

An aerial view of Hurst Castle and the Solent. (English Heritage)

Below left: Major Auxenfans and NCOs at the wartime garrison, Hurst Castle. (Hurst Castle)

Below right: A wartime searchlight on display in Hurst Castle grounds. (Maxine Knott)

There is a small and interesting museum at Hurst Castle. (Maxine Knott)

189

LEPE (Lepe Country Park, via A326)
There is a magnificent memorial here overlooking the Solent. This is the site of the PLUTO trials, and visitors can see the remains of Mulberry Harbour construction. Troops embarked from here for D-Day. The site has a visitor centre, and is open every day from 7.30am to 8pm or dusk, whichever is the earliest.
Lepe Country Park
Exbury
Southampton
Hampshire, SO45 1AD
023 8089 9108
lepe.enquiries@hants.gov.uk
www3.hants.gov.uk/lepe

LIME WOOD HOTEL, formerly Park Hill (B3056, Lyndhurst to Beaulieu road)
Park Hill was requisitioned by the NFS as a Regional HQ unit and was also used in planning for D-Day in 1944.
Lime Wood Hotel
Beaulieu Road
Lyndhurst
Hampshire, SO43 7FZ
023 8028 7177
info@limewood.co.ukhttp://www.limewoodhotel.co.uk/

LYMINGTON (via B3504, East End and Pylewell Park)
The site of a Second World War airfield. In the area are a surviving blister hangar and farm sheds that were used as debriefing rooms for returning air crew. These can be viewed from the road.

MINSTEAD
No. 716 Light Composite Company, Royal Army Service Corps was stationed in this village, south of Cadnam, on 6 August 1944 after returning from Normandy. This was an airborne unit. There is a silver alms dish in All Saints' Church (Church Lane) inscribed with the names of thirty-three men of this Company who died.

REFERENCES

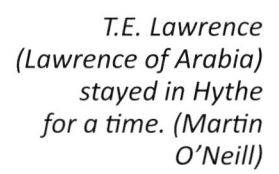

T.E. Lawrence (Lawrence of Arabia) stayed in Hythe for a time. (Martin O'Neill)

Map of the temporary airfield at Needs Oar Point. (James Kyle)

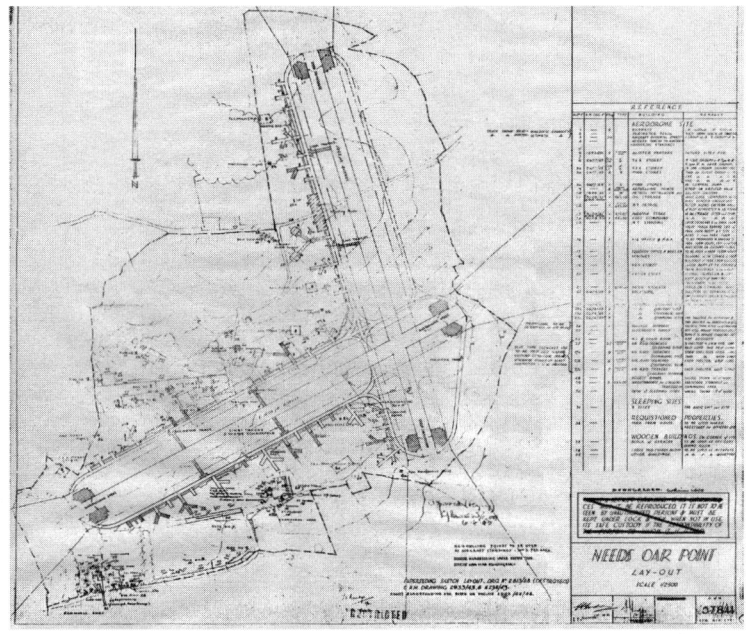

NEEDS OAR POINT (also referred to as Needs Ore Point; south of Beaulieu) One of the airfields of the New Forest, Typhoons flew from this often muddy site, which was protected by several AA batteries. The farmhouse at nearby Park Farm was an HQ unit. Along the shoreline are brick remains, and in some hedges on the farm are strips of Sommerfeld tracking: this was a lightweight wire mesh type of prefabricated airfield surface.
No access

A seagoing fireboat of the type used to protect craft around the Isle of Wight. (HFRS)

SETLEY PLAIN (A337, opposite The Filly Inn)

The site is between Brockenhurst and Lymington, off the A337. A few brick remains indicate the site of the former POW camp. Both German and Italian POWs, many of whom worked locally in agriculture, were held here at no. 65 Working Camp, Setley Plain, Brockenhurst. At least one of the German prisoners stayed behind and built a life in Ringwood after the war, and there is evidence to suggest at least ten former Setley POWs stayed in the United Kingdom rather than return home. The site is accessible.

REFERENCES

STONEY CROSS (via B3078)
Good evidence remains of this airfield, which was originally built on a 500-acre site, but was then expanded to 900 acres. There are views from the surrounding roads, or it is possible to walk some parts of the site – and even to turn up evidence.

SWAY
Quarr House is in Manchester Road, Sway. During the war it was no. 645 Camp for German POWs. The house has now been divided into flats.
No access

TOTTON (Testwood School, via A326)
Wartime use as a training centre for the Fire Service. Volunteer firefighters from Canada also trained here before supporting the NFS 1942–5.
No access

You are welcome to contact historian and author John Leete with relevant enquiries and for more information. Please email homefronthistory@btinternet.com or contact the publisher.
 All information included here is correct at the time of going to press.

The Unseen Legacy

A Second World War explosive device found by a walker in the New Forest has been blown up by bomb disposal experts. The bomb, thought to be an American shell, was discovered on Ibsley Common, Hampshire, on Wednesday by Trevor Vaughan after he sat down to rest. He said he put his compass down and noticed the needle swinging wildly. He said, 'I saw there was a little crater and I scraped away at the sandy earth, and there it was.' A Navy Bomb Disposal Team exploded the device. After finding it at Newlands Plantation on the common, Mr Vaughan called the National Trust, who notified the police. Ian Bradwell, the Trust's area warden for the New Forest, said, 'The device was in a remote part of the common, but we weren't taking any chances. We blocked off the tracks while the disposal unit dug a hole round it, sandbagged the area and blew it up.'

Mr Vaughan, who lives at Poulner near Ringwood, said he had been walking across Ibsley Common for about sixty years, since he was a boy. He said 'I did hear that an American aircraft came down around here during the war. Maybe it was something to do with that.'

Courtesy of BBC Hampshire and Isle of Wight News
For more stories please see
http://www.bbc.co.uk/news/uk-england-hampshire-24806535